WILDERNESS SURVIVAL HACKS

WILDERNESS SURVIVAL HACKS

THE ULTIMATE GUIDE TO CONQUERING THE WILDERNESS WITH EXPERT HACKS AND SKILLS

WILDERNESS MASTERY ESSENTIALS
BOOK 1

ALFRED GIBSON

Copyright © 2024 by Alfred Gibson

All rights reserved. No part of this book may be reproduced, stored in a retrieval system, or transmitted in any form or by any means, electronic, mechanical, photocopying, recording, or otherwise, without the prior written permission of the publisher, Book Bound Studios.

The information contained in this book is based on the author's personal experiences and research. While every effort has been made to ensure the accuracy of the information presented, the author and publisher cannot be held responsible for any errors or omissions.

This book is intended for general informational purposes only and is not a substitute for professional medical, legal, or financial advice. If you have specific questions about any medical, legal, or financial matters, you should consult with a qualified healthcare professional, attorney, or financial advisor.

Book Bound Studios is not affiliated with any product or vendor mentioned in this book. The views expressed in this book are those of the author and do not necessarily reflect the views of Book Bound Studios.

For the wild at heart and the brave of spirit, this book is dedicated to you. May the skills and knowledge within these pages guide you through your adventures, empower you to face the unpredictable, and inspire you to conquer the wilderness with confidence. To all who seek to understand the natural world and master the art of survival—this journey is yours.

In the wilderness, I find something more dear and connate than in streets or villages. In the tranquil landscape, and especially in the distant line of the horizon, man beholds somewhat as beautiful as his own nature.

— RALPH WALDO EMERSON

CONTENTS

Introduction to Wilderness Survival — xiii

1. BASIC SURVIVAL NEEDS — 1
   - Finding and Purifying Water — 1
   - Securing Food in the Wild — 3
   - Creating Shelter — 5
   - Maintaining Body Temperature — 8
   - Signaling for Help — 11
   - Chapter Summary — 14

2. NAVIGATION TECHNIQUES — 17
   - Using the Sun and Stars — 17
   - Understanding Maps and Compasses — 23
   - Landmarks and Natural Indicators — 25
   - Making and Using a Makeshift Compass — 27
   - Chapter Summary — 29

3. FIRECRAFT — 33
   - Basics of Starting a Fire — 33
   - Fire Starting Materials and Tinder — 36
   - Building a Fire for Heat and Cooking — 38
   - Signaling with Fire — 40
   - Extinguishing Fires Safely — 43
   - Chapter Summary — 45

4. FORAGING FOR FOOD — 47
   - Identifying Edible Plants — 47
   - Avoiding Poisonous Plants — 50
   - Foraging Techniques — 52
   - Hunting and Trapping Small Game — 54

Preparing Wild Food	56
Chapter Summary	59
5. FIRST AID AND HEALTH	**61**
Handling Bites and Stings	61
Natural Remedies	65
Preventing and Treating Hypothermia and Heatstroke	67
Mental Health and Coping Mechanisms	69
Chapter Summary	72
6. SURVIVAL GEAR ESSENTIALS	**75**
The Survival Kit	75
Choosing the Right Tools	78
DIY Survival Gear	80
Maintaining Your Gear	82
Innovative Uses for Common Items	85
Chapter Summary	87
7. WATER CROSSINGS AND TRAVEL	**89**
Crossing Rivers Safely	89
Building Rafts and Floats	91
Swimming in Open Water	93
Dealing with Marine Hazards	95
Conserving Energy During Travel	97
Chapter Summary	100
8. WEATHER AND ENVIRONMENT	**103**
Predicting Weather Patterns	103
Surviving in Extreme Conditions	106
Adapting to Different Environments	108
Impact of Climate Change on Survival	111
Chapter Summary	113
9. SURVIVAL PSYCHOLOGY	**115**
Staying Calm Under Pressure	115
The Will to Survive	118

Decision-Making in Crisis Situations	120
Group Dynamics and Leadership	122
Coping with Isolation and Fear	125
Chapter Summary	128
10. ADVANCED SURVIVAL TECHNIQUES	131
Improvised Weapons and Tools	131
Constructing Long-Term Shelters	135
Advanced Navigation Challenges	137
Living Off the Land	139
Self-Rescue Strategies	141
Chapter Summary	144
The Journey Ahead	147
Your Feedback Matters	159
About the Author	161

INTRODUCTION TO WILDERNESS SURVIVAL

A set of tools scattered along the wilderness floor.

The Importance of Being Prepared

Venturing into the wilderness, whether for leisure, adventure or in an unforeseen survival situation, demands a level of preparedness that cannot be overstated. The difference between a memorable adventure and a dangerous ordeal often hinges on the degree of preparation undertaken before setting foot into the great outdoors. The start of this book delves into the critical importance of being prepared, offering insights and strategies to ensure you are well-equipped to face the challenges and unpredictabilities of the wilderness.

Preparation for wilderness survival begins with a mindset that embraces planning, knowledge acquisition, and practical skill development. The first step is understanding that the wilderness does not conform to our expectations but demands respect and caution. It's about recognizing that while the wilderness offers beauty and tranquility, it also presents dangers, from unpredictable weather to potentially hazardous terrain and wildlife encounters.

One of the foundational aspects of being prepared is having a comprehensive understanding of the environment you're entering. This involves researching the area you plan to visit, including its climate, topography, potential hazards, and any recent changes or events that might impact your visit (such as forest fires, floods, or wildlife activity). With this knowledge, you can better plan your trip, including selecting the most appropriate routes, campsites, and times of year to visit.

Equally important is equipping yourself with the necessary gear and supplies. This doesn't mean overburdening yourself with every conceivable gadget but carefully selecting items that are essential for survival and safety. Key items include a reliable means of communication, navigation tools (such as a map and compass or GPS device), a first-aid kit, a multi-purpose tool, fire-starting materials, and adequate food and water supplies. It's also crucial to have appropriate clothing and shelter tailored to the specific conditions you expect to encounter to protect against the elements.

Beyond physical preparations, mental readiness plays a pivotal role in wilderness survival. This encompasses having a positive and resilient mindset and being equipped with essential survival skills. Knowing how to find and purify water, build a shelter, signal for help, navigate without a compass, and identify edible plants can make the difference between life and death. Regularly practicing these skills in a controlled environment can boost your confidence and competence, making you better prepared to face unexpected situations.

Finally, preparation also means having a clear plan and communicating it with others. Inform someone trustworthy about your itinerary, including where you're going, the routes you plan to take, and when you expect to return. This simple step can be lifesaving, ensuring that rescuers have a starting point to begin their search if something goes awry.

In essence, preparing for wilderness survival is about adopting a comprehensive approach combining knowledge, skills, and practical measures. It's about foreseeing potential challenges and equipping yourself to meet them head-on. With the proper preparation, the wilderness can be a source of immense joy and profound experiences rather than a setting for survival struggles. As we move forward, understanding the wilderness's complexity and unpredictability becomes the next crucial step in our journey of preparedness and survival.

Understanding the Wilderness

Going into the wild requires more than just a robust spirit and a backpack full of gear. It demands a deep understanding of the environment you're entering. The wilderness, with its vast landscapes and untamed nature, is both beautiful and unforgiving. To navigate its challenges, one must first appreciate its complexity and learn to read the subtle cues it provides.

Introduction to Wilderness Survival

The wilderness varies greatly from dense forests and arid deserts to towering mountains and expansive plains. Each ecosystem presents its unique set of challenges and resources. Understanding these environments is crucial for practical survival. For instance, finding water in a desert requires different strategies than in a rainforest. Similarly, the materials available for shelter or fire-making can vastly differ between a snowy tundra and a temperate forest.

Weather plays a significant role in wilderness survival. Conditions can change rapidly, turning a manageable situation into a difficult one. Knowing weather patterns and the ability to read the sky can make the difference between staying dry and warm or suffering from exposure. Preparing for the worst-case scenario, such as unexpected storms or extreme temperatures, is part of understanding the wilderness.

Wildlife is another critical aspect. The wilderness is home to various creatures, each adapted to survive in specific environments. Learning about the local fauna, including which animals are dangerous and which can provide food, is essential. Additionally, understanding animal behavior can prevent unwanted encounters and help source food in survival situations.

Navigation skills are indispensable in the wilderness. Modern technology, like GPS, has made it

Introduction to Wilderness Survival

easier to find our way, but these devices can fail. A deep understanding of traditional navigation methods, such as using a compass and reading topographical maps, ensures that one can always find their way. Moreover, natural navigation techniques, such as using the position of the sun, stars, and even certain plant species, can enhance one's ability to move through the wilderness confidently.

Finally, the psychological aspect of wilderness survival must be balanced. Understanding the wilderness also means understanding oneself. It's about knowing your limits, managing fear, and staying calm in adversity. The wilderness can be isolating, and the mental challenges often outweigh the physical ones. Developing resilience, maintaining a positive attitude, and practicing mindfulness can significantly impact survival outcomes.

Understanding the wilderness is about respecting its power and learning to coexist with nature. It's a comprehensive approach that combines knowledge of the environment, skills in navigation and survival techniques, and psychological preparedness. This foundation prepares one for the challenges of wilderness survival. It enriches the experience, allowing for a deeper connection with the natural world. As we progress, we'll delve into the essential survival skills that build upon this understanding, equipping you with the tools needed to thrive in the wilderness.

Essential Survival Skills Overview

Travelling through the wilderness demands a foundational understanding of essential survival skills. These skills are the bedrock upon which all wilderness survival knowledge is built, equipping you with the tools necessary to navigate, endure, and ultimately thrive in the natural environment. This overview serves as a bridge from grasping the vast and varied aspects of the wilderness to preparing your mind and body for its challenges.

First and foremost, the ability to find and purify water is paramount. Water is life, and understanding how to locate water sources, whether by recognizing terrain features that suggest the presence of water or by collecting dew and rainwater, can make the difference between survival and succumbing to dehydration. Equally important is knowing how to purify water using boiling, chemical treatment, or filtration methods to remove pathogens that can cause illness.

Next, mastering the skill of building a shelter is critical for protection against the elements. A shelter can shield you from the harsh sun, insulate you against

Introduction to Wilderness Survival

cold, and provide a barrier from wind and rain. The type of shelter you build will depend on the resources available in your environment and the specific conditions you are facing. Learning several methods for constructing shelters using natural materials or items from a survival kit can significantly increase your chances of enduring adverse conditions.

Fire-making is another indispensable skill. Fire serves multiple purposes: to keep you warm, cook food, purify water, signal for help, and deter wildlife. Familiarity with various fire-starting techniques, including using a spark, friction, or the sun's rays with a lens, is crucial. Equally important is understanding how to gather and prepare tinder, kindling, and fuel to sustain a fire under different weather conditions.

Foraging for food is a skill that requires knowledge and caution. The wilderness is home to a plethora of edible plants, insects, and animals, but also to many that are toxic. Identifying safe, nutritious food sources and basic trapping and fishing techniques can sustain you over extended periods. This knowledge not only aids in survival but deepens your connection to the natural world.

Lastly, navigation skills are essential to find your way in the wilderness. Familiarity with reading topographic maps, using a compass, and understanding natural navigation cues such as the position of the sun and stars can help you orient yourself and plan your movements. In today's digital age, proficiency with GPS devices is beneficial. Still, it's vital to prepare for scenarios where technology may fail.

As we transition from understanding the wilderness to preparing ourselves mentally and physically, remember that these essential survival skills form the foundation of that preparation. They empower us to survive and thrive in the natural world, fostering a deep respect for its beauty and challenges.

Mental and Physical Preparation

Embarking on a wilderness adventure, whether by choice or circumstance, demands more than just a backpack full of gear and a map. The real journey begins with the mental and physical preparation that sets the foundation for survival. This section delves into the crucial aspects of preparing oneself mentally and physically before stepping into the wild, ensuring you are as ready as can be for whatever nature throws your way.

Mental Preparation: The Bedrock of Survival

Introduction to Wilderness Survival

The wilderness does not discriminate. It is an impartial teacher that presents challenges and lessons in equal measure. Mental resilience, therefore, becomes your most valuable asset. Start by cultivating a positive mindset. Believe in your ability to overcome challenges and remind yourself that adversity is not a roadblock but a stepping stone to growth. Try to familiarize yourself with common survival scenarios and visualize yourself navigating them successfully. This mental rehearsal boosts confidence and reduces panic in real-life situations.

Stress management is another critical aspect of mental preparation. Learn techniques such as deep breathing, meditation, or mindfulness to keep anxiety at bay. The ability to remain calm under pressure can significantly influence your decision-making process and survival chances.

Physical Preparation: Building the Temple

Survival is a physical endeavor as much as it is a mental one. Begin by assessing your physical condition and identify areas for improvement. Cardiovascular endurance, strength, and flexibility are paramount. Incorporate running, swimming, or cycling into your routine to boost stamina. Strength training, focusing on functional movements, prepares your body for the rigors of outdoor activities like climbing, lifting, and carrying. Flexibility exercises, such as yoga or stretching routines, enhance mobility and reduce the risk of injury.

Equally important is familiarizing yourself with the physical demands of specific environments. For example, if you're heading to a mountainous area, include hikes in your training to acclimate your body to the elevation and terrain. For cold environments, practice with the gear you'll be using, such as snowshoes or skis, to ensure comfort and proficiency.

Your body's performance is heavily influenced by what you consume. Prioritize a balanced diet rich in nutrients to support your physical training. Hydration is equally crucial; learn to manage your water intake and recognize the signs of dehydration. Understanding the basics of wilderness nutrition, such as identifying edible plants or purifying water, can be lifesaving.

Lastly, always appreciate the power of rest and recovery. Adequate sleep and rest days are essential for physical and mental recovery, reducing the risk of burnout and injury. Learn to listen to your body and give it the care it deserves.

As you gear up for your wilderness adventure, remember that the journey begins long before you set foot on the trail. Mental and physical preparation are the cornerstones of survival, equipping you with the resilience, strength, and wisdom to face the challenges ahead. With these foundations in place, you're ready to embark on a journey of discovery, learning, and growth in the great outdoors.

1

BASIC SURVIVAL NEEDS

A tent and campfire in the wilderness.

Finding and Purifying Water

Securing a safe water source is paramount for survival. The human body can only last a few days without water, making it a critical first step in survival. When searching for water, look for natural formations such as valleys and low-lying areas where water naturally collects. Rivers, streams, and lakes are obvious sources, but pay attention to morning dew or rainwater, which can be collected with a clean cloth or container. Be cautious of stagnant water or sources near animal tracks to avoid contamination.

Once you've found a water source, purification is the next crucial step, as natural water can contain harmful pathogens. Boiling is the most effective method to purify water. Bring the water to a rolling boil for at least one minute, longer at higher altitudes, to kill bacteria, viruses, and parasites. If boiling is not an option, chemical purifiers like iodine or chlorine tablets can be used. However, they may leave an aftertaste and are ineffective against all pathogens. Filtering through a clean cloth can remove large particulates before boiling or chemical treatment. Still, on its own, more is needed to ensure safety.

Solar water disinfection (SODIS) can be a viable alternative in situations where none of these methods are available. Fill a clear plastic bottle with water and place it in direct sunlight for at least six hours. The UV rays will help inactivate most pathogens, making drinking water safer. Remember, while these methods can significantly reduce the risk of waterborne diseases, none are foolproof, and caution should always be exercised when drinking water in the wilderness.

Securing Food in the Wild

After ensuring you have access to clean water, the next critical step in wilderness survival is securing food. While the prospect of finding and preparing food in the wild may seem daunting, you can employ several practical strategies to nourish yourself until help arrives or you find your way back to civilization.

First, it's essential to understand the environment you're in, as different ecosystems offer various food sources. Forests, for example, are rich in nuts, berries, and mushrooms, but not all are safe to eat. Identifying a few common, edible plants before your adventure can be lifesaving. Deserts, while seemingly barren, can provide plants like cacti that contain water and nutrients and insects high in protein.

Foraging is often the most accessible means of securing food, but caution is paramount. Always avoid plants with milky sap, a bitter taste, or an almond scent when crushed, as these can be indicators of toxicity. Stick to fruits and vegetables that you recognize, such as dandelions, which are entirely edible, or easily identifiable berries like blackberries. The rule of thumb is: when in doubt, leave it out.

Insects and small animals can also be excellent protein sources. Insects such as crickets, grasshoppers, and ants are widely available and can be eaten raw or cooked. However, avoid brightly colored insects or those that emit a strong odor, as these characteristics can indicate toxicity. Small fish, frogs, and snakes can be caught using simple traps or makeshift fishing gear, but cooking these animals is crucial to kill potential pathogens.

Fishing can be a viable option if you find yourself near a water source. Using a safety pin or a makeshift hook, you can fashion a fishing line from your survival kit's thread or string. Bait can be anything from small insects to pieces of fruit. Patience and stillness are your allies here, as fish are easily startled by sudden movements.

Regardless of your food source, safety should always be your top priority. Ensure all food, especially meat, is cooked thoroughly to avoid foodborne illnesses. If you're unsure about the edibility of a plant or fungus, performing a simple contact test on your skin can help determine its safety. Remember, securing food is about sustenance, not gourmet dining. Focus on calorie-rich foods that will provide you with the energy to survive.

While survival is your primary goal, respecting nature and conserving resources is also essential. Take only what you need and leave the environment as undisturbed as possible. This not only ensures that the ecosystem remains balanced, but it also leaves resources for other survivors who may come after you.

Creating a shelter will be your focus in the next steps of your survival journey. A secure and safe shelter can protect you from the elements and improve your chances of survival. But for now, remember that securing food, while challenging, is entirely feasible with the proper knowledge and a bit of ingenuity.

Creating Shelter

After addressing the crucial aspect of securing food, the following fundamental step is creating shelter. The shelter protects from the elements and psychological comfort that can be vital in survival situations. The art of creating a shelter using the resources available in the wild is both a skill and a craft that can significantly increase your chances of survival.

The first step in creating a shelter is to choose the correct location. Look for a dry spot, elevated and protected from the wind. Avoid areas prone to natural hazards such as flooding, falling rocks, or heavy snow accumulations. Once you've found a suitable location, assess the materials available. The natural environment can provide a wealth of resources, from branches and leaves to snow and mud, depending on the climate and terrain.

A lean-to is one of the simplest yet most effective shelters you can construct. Start by finding a long, sturdy branch to serve as the ridgepole—the backbone of your lean-to. Prop one end of the ridgepole up on a tree or a couple of sturdy branches wedged into the ground. Then, lean smaller branches against the ridgepole at an angle to create a framework. Finally, layer the framework with smaller branches, leaves, and other insulating materials to protect against wind and rain. The lean-to should be built just enough to accommodate you, as a smaller space is more accessible to keep warm.

Wilderness Survival Hacks

A simple lean-to shelter.

A snow cave can be a lifesaver if you're in a snowy environment. Begin by finding a drift of deep, stable snow. Using a digging tool or your hands, excavate a tunnel into a small chamber. As cold air sinks, the chamber should be carved out so that the sleeping platform is higher than the entrance. Compact the snow around the chamber to strengthen the structure and smooth the interior walls to prevent dripping. A small ventilation hole at the top is crucial to ensure a supply of fresh air.

Your creativity and resourcefulness are your best allies in environments where materials are scarce. A debris hut, for example, can be constructed with minimal resources. Start by creating a frame with a long central spine and ribs resembling a fish's frame. Cover this framework with whatever debris is available—leaves, grass, and small branches—to create insulation and waterproofing. The entrance should be small to conserve heat and, if possible, create a door with additional debris.

Remember, the primary purpose of your shelter is to protect you from the elements and retain body heat. As such, insulation is critical. Use leaves, grasses, pine needles, or even your spare clothing to insulate the floor of your shelter and keep you off the cold ground. In colder climates, the thickness of your insulation can make the difference between a cold, sleepless night and restful warmth.

Creating a shelter in the wilderness is more than survival; it's about using the environment to your advantage, respecting nature's resources, and ensuring your safety until you can reach help or make it out on your own. With practice and knowledge, the ability to create a shelter can empower you to face the challenges of the wild with confidence.

Maintaining Body Temperature

In the wilderness, your ability to maintain an optimal body temperature can mean the difference between a challenging adventure and a life-threatening ordeal. The human body operates within a narrow temperature range, and when exposed to the extremes of the wilderness, maintaining this balance becomes a critical survival skill.

First and foremost, understanding the basics of how your body loses heat is essential. There are four primary ways:

- **Conduction** (transfer of heat through direct contact with objects).
- **Convection** (losing heat to the surrounding air cooler than your body).
- **Evaporation** (loss of heat as sweat evaporates from your skin).
- **Radiation** (emission of heat from your body to your surroundings).

Knowing these principles, you can employ several hacks to maintain your body temperature effectively.

Layering your clothing is a fundamental strategy. It's not just about piling on as many clothes as possible but about understanding the function of each layer:

- A moisture-wicking base layer to keep your skin dry.
- An insulating layer to trap body heat.

- A waterproof and windproof outer layer to protect against the elements.

This system allows you to adjust your insulation according to activity level and the weather, preventing overheating and hypothermia.

In cold conditions, your head and extremities are particularly vulnerable to heat loss. Wearing a hat or a balaclava can significantly reduce heat escape from your head. At the same time, gloves and woolen socks protect your hands and feet. Consider stuffing your jacket or pants with dry leaves, grass, or newspaper in extreme cold for additional insulation. This might seem unconventional, but such improvisation can be lifesaving in a survival situation.

Staying dry is another crucial aspect of maintaining body temperature. Wet clothing loses its insulating properties and can lead to rapid heat loss through conduction. If you fall into the water or your clothes get wet from rain or sweat, prioritize finding shelter and changing into dry clothes if available. When you can't change, try to wring out your clothes as much as possible and use your body heat to dry them.

At night, the challenge of staying warm intensifies as temperatures drop. If you've managed to create a shelter, the next step is to build a bed that insulates you from the ground. A simple bed can be made from branches, leaves, or pine needles. The goal is to create a barrier that minimizes heat loss to the ground through conduction. Additionally, using a fire for warmth is a classic survival technique. However, ensuring your shelter is well-ventilated is crucial to avoid carbon monoxide poisoning.

Lastly, remember that your body needs fuel to generate heat. Consuming high-energy foods and staying hydrated helps your body maintain its core temperature. Even simple actions like sipping warm water or hot tea can boost a significant warmth from the inside out.

As we transition from the necessity of creating a shelter to the importance of signaling for help, remember that maintaining your body temperature is not just about comfort but survival. The strategies outlined here are designed to keep you alive and functional, enabling you to take the following steps toward rescue and safety.

Signaling for Help

Having discussed the importance of maintaining body temperature in a survival situation, it's equally vital to understand how to signal for help effectively. Being stranded in the wilderness is daunting, but knowing how to attract the attention of rescuers can significantly increase your chances of survival. This section delves into practical and innovative ways to signal for help when lost or distressed.

Ensuring visibility is the first principle in signaling for help. Bright colors stand out against the natural backdrop, so if you have any brightly colored clothing or materials, use them to your advantage. Lay them out in an open area or tie them to a high point to catch the eye of passing rescuers.

Smoking is one of the most traditional yet effective methods to signal for help. A fire serves multiple survival purposes, but with the proper technique, it can also be a powerful signal. Add green vegetation, rubber, or oil to your fire to create visible smoke during the day. This produces thick, white smoke that can be seen for miles. A bright fire is visible from a great distance at night, so focus on maintaining an intense blaze.

Reflective objects can be lifesavers in signaling for help. When it catches the sun, the flash of a mirror can be seen from far away, even by aircraft. If you don't have a mirror, any reflective surface, such as a piece of aluminum foil, a CD, or even the shiny side of a survival blanket, can work. Practice aiming the reflection toward your intended target for maximum effect.

Sound can be your best ally when visibility is low, or you're in dense foliage. Three loud, evenly spaced noises (blows on a whistle, gunshots, or even banging rocks together) are universally recognized as a distress signal. Repeat this signal at regular intervals to help rescuers locate you.

In open spaces, creating prominent symbols on the ground can attract the attention of search planes. Use rocks, logs, or even make trenches in the soil to spell out "SOS" or "HELP." Make sure these symbols are as large and contrasted against the environment to be visible from the air.

Finally, while it might seem counterintuitive, staying in one place increases your chances of being found. A moving target is more challenging to locate. Hence, you need to be sure of your direction to create a base where you can signal for help, maintain your basic needs, and wait for rescue.

Incorporating these signaling techniques into your survival strategy can dramatically increase your visibility and the likelihood of being rescued. Remember, the goal is to make it as easy as possible for rescuers to find you, so use these methods wisely and persistently.

Chapter Summary

- Understanding your environment is crucial for finding food in the wilderness, with different ecosystems offering varied resources like nuts, berries, game, and fish.
- Foraging for plant-based foods requires knowledge to distinguish between edible and toxic plants, focusing on universally edible plants like dandelions and cattails.
- Hunting and trapping can provide protein through small game or larger animals if one has the necessary skills and patience.
- Fishing, using improvised gear like a branch for a pole or creating simple traps, offers a safer alternative for food, as fish are less likely to carry diseases affecting humans.
- Safety is paramount when securing food in the wild, including cooking food thoroughly and avoiding consumption of unidentified plants or animals.
- Conservation and respect for nature are emphasized, taking only what is needed and minimizing environmental impact to preserve resources for future generations.

- Shelter creation is a crucial survival skill, with different techniques suited to various environments, from lean-tos in forests to snow caves in snowy conditions.
- Maintaining body temperature through strategies like layering clothing, staying dry, and building insulated shelters is critical, as is signaling for help using visual and auditory signals to increase chances of rescue.

2

NAVIGATION TECHNIQUES

An explorer using a compass and map at night.

Using the Sun and Stars

In the vast and unpredictable wilderness, the sun and stars are not just celestial bodies that light up the sky;

they are ancient navigational tools that have guided explorers and adventurers through the ages. Understanding how to use these natural phenomena for navigation can be a lifesaver when modern technology fails or is unavailable. This section delves into practical techniques for using the sun and stars to find your way in the wilderness.

Navigating by the Sun

The sun rises in the east and sets in the west - a fundamental principle that can help orient you in the wilderness. During the day, the sun's position can give you a general sense of direction. The Shadow-Tip Method is a straightforward method to find your direction, which involves using a stick and the sun to find the north.

1. Place a stick vertically into the ground to cast a shadow.
2. Mark the tip of the shadow with a stone or any small object. This marks the west direction.
3. Wait about 15 minutes, and you'll notice the shadow moves.

4. Mark the new position of the shadow tip. This marks the east direction.
5. Draw a line between the two marks to get an east-west line. Standing with the first mark (west) to your left and the second mark (east) to your right, you are now facing north.

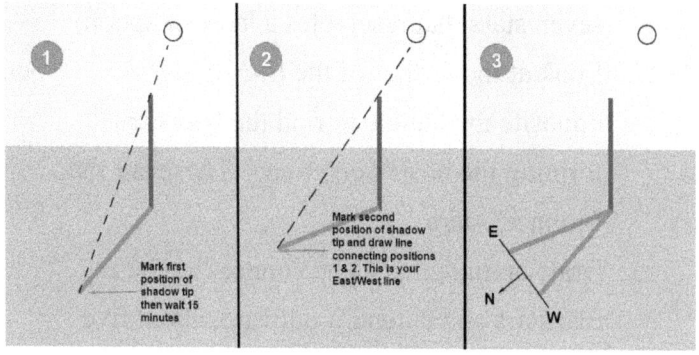

The Shadow-Tip Method by @AlamoAreaBSA.

This method is most effective around noon when the sun is at its highest point in the sky. It's a quick way to establish cardinal directions. It can be instrumental in open areas where the sun is visible.

Navigating by the Stars

At night, the stars take over as guides. Polaris, also

known as the North Star, is the most well-known navigation star. It's almost directly above the North Pole, making it a reliable north indicator in the Northern Hemisphere.

To find Polaris:

1. Locate the Big Dipper, a prominent group of seven stars that resembles a ladle or spoon.
2. Look at the "edge" of the Big Dipper opposite the handle to find the two stars forming the bowl's outer part. These are the "pointer" stars.
3. Draw an imaginary line connecting these two stars and extend it outward, about five times the distance between them.
4. This line points directly to Polaris, the last star in the handle of the Little Dipper.

Wilderness Survival Hacks

Polaris in the night sky by Science Sparks.

The Southern Cross (Crux) is a crucial constellation for finding south in the Southern Hemisphere. Extending an imaginary line from the top to the bottom of the Southern Cross and projecting it towards the horizon can approximate the south direction.

The Southern Cross by The Nine Planets.

Practical Tips

- Practice these methods before you need them. Familiarity with the sun's path and the night sky will make navigation much easier when the situation arises.
- Remember that environmental factors like mountains, valleys, and dense forests can affect your perception of the sun's position and the visibility of stars. Always cross-check with other navigation methods if possible.
- Remember the seasonal variations in the sun's path and the visibility of constellations. The more you understand these patterns, the more accurately you can navigate.

By mastering these ancient techniques of using the sun and stars for navigation, you equip yourself with valuable skills that enhance your wilderness survival toolkit. While modern navigation tools are convenient and precise, the reliability and universality of celestial navigation make it an indispensable backup method for any adventurer.

Understanding Maps and Compasses

Mastering the art of navigation is akin to holding the key to your safety and direction. While the celestial bodies offer a natural compass, the tools of the modern explorer—maps and compasses—provide precision and reliability that can be lifesaving in unfamiliar terrains. This section delves into the foundational skills of understanding and utilizing these indispensable tools.

Maps are not merely pieces of paper adorned with lines and symbols; they are comprehensive guides to the landscape, detailing topography, water sources, trails, and other critical landmarks. To effectively use a map, one must first become familiar with its scale, which indicates the relationship between distances on the map and the actual distances on the ground. Understanding scale is crucial for estimating travel times and distances. Learning to interpret the various symbols and colors is essential for identifying natural features, artificial structures, and other critical navigational aids.

Complementing the map, the compass serves as the navigator's steadfast ally, offering direction when landmarks are invisible or when darkness veils the path. The essential skill of aligning the compass needle with the magnetic north allows travelers to establish their bearing—a fundamental step in navigating from one point to another. However, the true art of compass use involves more nuanced skills, such as "taking a bearing," which enables one to determine the direction of a specific landmark or feature on the map. This technique involves aligning the compass with the desired destination on the map and then translating that direction into the physical environment.

The synergy between map and compass is where the magic of navigation unfolds. By placing the compass on the map and aligning it with the map's orientation and the landscape, adventurers can chart a course through the wilderness, making adjustments as necessary based on the terrain and other factors. This method, known as "triangulation," can also help pinpoint one's current location using visible landmarks and their corresponding map representations.

While technology offers modern tools such as GPS devices, the fundamental skills of map and compass navigation remain invaluable. Electronic devices can fail due to battery depletion, damage, or signal loss, making traditional navigation skills an essential backup. Moreover, manually charting a course and connecting with the landscape fosters a deeper understanding and appreciation of the natural world.

As we transition from the celestial guidance of the sun and stars to the earthbound cues of landmarks and natural indicators, the importance of a well-rounded navigational skill set becomes clear. The ability to read the land and sky, interpret maps, and utilize a compass forms a comprehensive toolkit that empowers the wilderness explorer to venture confidently into the unknown, secure in the knowledge that they possess the skills to find their way.

Landmarks and Natural Indicators

In the wilderness, where modern navigation tools might not always be available, understanding how to use landmarks and natural indicators can be a lifesaver. This section delves into the art of navigating by observing the natural environment. This skill has guided explorers and indigenous peoples long before the invention of the compass and GPS.

Landmarks are distinctive features in the landscape that can help you orient yourself and navigate from one place to another. These can be anything from a uniquely shaped tree, a large rock formation, a mountain peak, or even an artificial structure like a tower or building visible from a distance. The key to effectively using landmarks is to choose unmistakable and visible features from afar. When you identify a landmark, it's crucial to note its direction about your current position. Keep the landmark in sight as you move to maintain your sense of direction.

However, the wilderness often requires more than just landmark navigation, especially in dense forests or areas with scarce distinctive features. This is where natural indicators come into play. Nature provides its navigation tools if you know where to look.

The Sun: The most apparent natural indicator is the sun. Rising in the east and setting in the west, the sun can provide a general sense of direction. In the northern hemisphere, the sun will be due south in the middle of the day, while in the southern hemisphere, it will be due north.

The Moon and Stars: At night, the moon and stars serve as celestial guides. The North Star (Polaris) remains fixed in the northern sky and directly aligns with the Earth's rotational axis. Finding Polaris can help you determine the north direction. If the moon rises before sunset, its illuminated side will face west; if it rises after midnight, its illuminated side will face east.

Vegetation: Plants can also indicate direction. In the northern hemisphere, moss tends to grow on the northern side of trees because it prefers shaded, moist environments. Similarly, trees with thicker branches on one side often indicate the direction of the prevailing wind, which can be another clue to orientation.

Water Flow: In many landscapes, rivers and streams flow in a consistent direction, often towards more significant bodies of water. By understanding the local geography, you can use the direction of water flow to guide your path.

Mastering landmarks and natural indicators for navigation requires practice and attentiveness to the environment. By developing these skills, you can enhance your ability to move through the wilderness confidently, even when modern navigation tools are not an option. As we progress, we'll explore how to refine your navigation skills by making and using makeshift tools, ensuring you're never truly lost in the wild.

Making and Using a Makeshift Compass

In the heart of the wilderness, where the modern conveniences of GPS and digital compasses are beyond reach, the savvy survivor must return to the roots of ancient navigation. One ingenious and surprisingly simple method involves creating a makeshift compass. This technique can be a game-changer for those disoriented among nature's vast expanses.

To begin, you'll need to find a small, flat surface

that can float on water—a leaf, a piece of bark, or even a paper scrap if you have one. Next, locate a needle or a thin, straight piece of metal. A small, straight twig can serve as a rudimentary substitute in a pinch, though it's less than ideal.

The magic ingredient in this survival hack is magnetism. By magnetizing the needle, you give it the properties needed to align with the Earth's magnetic field, turning it into a compass needle. To magnetize your needle, you can use silk or wool fabric. If you're wearing a cotton shirt, the friction from vigorously rubbing the needle across your clothing might also do the trick, albeit less effectively. Running the needle through your hair several times can also magnetize it without fabric, thanks to the static electricity generated.

Once magnetized, place your needle gently on the flat surface you've prepared. This makeshift raft then needs to be set afloat on still water. A small puddle, a calm pond, or even a cupped hand filled with water can serve as your navigational arena. The key is to ensure that the water is as motionless as possible to prevent artificial movement of the needle.

As the needle settles, it will slowly orient itself along the north-south axis, with one end pointing towards the magnetic north. It's important to note that

Wilderness Survival Hacks

this method indicates magnetic north, which can vary slightly from true north depending on your global location. However, in a survival situation, this distinction is often a minor concern compared to the immediate need to establish a general direction.

You can now start making informed decisions about your movement using your makeshift compass. By knowing north, you can deduce the other cardinal directions—east, west, and south—and choose your path accordingly. While not as precise as modern navigational tools, this method can provide a crucial advantage in finding your way to safety or reaching a destination when other means are unavailable.

Remember, the effectiveness of a makeshift compass can be influenced by nearby magnetic fields generated by large metal objects, so it's wise to use this method in a clear area away from potential interference. With practice, creating and using a makeshift compass can become a valuable skill in your wilderness survival toolkit, bridging the gap between ancient wisdom and modern survival techniques.

Chapter Summary

- The sun and stars have been used for navigation in the wilderness for ages, offering a reliable method when modern technology is unavailable.
- The Shadow-Tip Method utilizes a stick and the sun to find north by marking the shadow's movement, effective around noon.
- Polaris (the North Star) indicates north in the Northern Hemisphere at night, found by extending a line from the Big Dipper's pointer stars.
- In the Southern Hemisphere, the Southern Cross constellation helps find south by extending a line from its top to bottom toward the horizon.
- Maps and compasses provide precision in navigation, with skills in reading map scales and symbols and using a compass to find bearings essential.
- Landmarks and natural indicators like the sun's position, moon phases, star positions, and vegetation growth offer guidance without tools.

- A makeshift compass can be created with a magnetized needle and a floating surface in water, pointing towards magnetic north.
- Natural navigation techniques include observing the sun's movement, moon phases, stars like Polaris, and following rivers or streams, requiring practice and attention to detail.

3
FIRECRAFT

A campfire in the wilderness surrounded by five campers.

Basics of Starting a Fire

Mastering the art of firecraft begins with understanding the basics of starting a fire. This skill is a cornerstone of wilderness survival and a gateway to warmth, safety, and comfort in the great outdoors. Igniting a flame in the wilderness might seem daunting at first. Still, it becomes an achievable task with the proper knowledge and techniques.

The first step in starting a fire is selecting an appropriate site. Look for a location sheltered from the wind yet well-ventilated to ensure the smoke doesn't become a nuisance. It's crucial to clear the area of any debris, dry leaves, or anything that could catch fire unintentionally. Creating a small pit or ring of rocks can help contain the fire and reduce its impact on the surrounding environment.

Once the site is prepared, the next step is gathering materials. Fire needs three elements to thrive: **heat**, **fuel**, and **oxygen**. These elements form the "fire triangle," a concept essential for successful fire starting. The initial focus should be collecting tinder, which consists of small, easily ignitable materials that catch fire with minimal heat. Examples include dry leaves, grass, pine needles, or even lint from your pockets.

Following tinder, kindling is the next type of material to gather. Kindling consists of small sticks and twigs that can catch fire from the burning tinder. Kindling aims to build a small, steady flame to ignite larger wood pieces. Choosing kindling that's dry and snaps easily is essential, as moisture can hinder its ability to burn.

The final step in the preparation phase is collecting fuel wood. These larger pieces of wood will keep the fire burning for an extended period. When selecting fuel wood, aim for dry pieces roughly the size of your wrist or larger. Avoid using green or freshly cut wood, as it contains moisture that makes it difficult to burn.

With all the materials gathered, it's time to assemble the fire. A popular method is the teepee structure, where kindling is arranged in a cone shape around the tinder. This setup allows air to circulate freely, feeding oxygen to the flames. Once the structure is in place, the next step is to ignite the tinder. This can be done using matches, a lighter, or even a fire starter if you're practicing primitive firecraft techniques.

As the tinder catches fire, gently blow on the base of the flame to provide additional oxygen, which will help the fire grow. Once the kindling begins to burn, gradually add larger pieces of fuel wood, careful not to smother the flames. The fire will become self-sufficient with patience and careful attention, providing warmth, light, and a means to cook food.

Starting a fire in the wilderness is a skill that embodies the essence of survival and self-reliance. By understanding the basics of firecraft, you're not only preparing yourself for the challenges of the wild but also connecting with an ancient practice that has been essential to human survival for millennia.

Fire Starting Materials and Tinder

After understanding the basics of starting a fire, it's crucial to delve deeper into the materials that can transform a spark into a blaze: fire-starting materials and tinder. This section aims to equip you with the knowledge to identify and utilize various natural and man-made materials that can be your best allies in igniting a fire under challenging conditions.

Tinder is the foundation of building a fire. It consists of any material that catches fire easily and burns quickly. The right tinder can distinguish between warmth and hypothermia, light and darkness in the wilderness. Natural tinders are abundant in the wild; you must know where to look. Dry leaves, grass, and pine needles can serve as excellent tinder, provided they are completely dry. Birch bark, with its natural oils, can catch fire even when damp. Another invaluable resource is deadwood, specifically the tiny twigs and branches that snap off easily, indicating their dryness.

Carrying your tinder can be a game-changer for those who like to come prepared. Cotton balls soaked in petroleum jelly, dryer lint, or even finely shredded paper can be compact, lightweight additions to your survival kit. These materials catch fire quickly and sustain a flame long enough to ignite larger pieces of kindling.

Moving beyond tinder, kindling is the next step in building your fire. Kindling consists of slightly larger materials than tinder, such as small sticks and branches, which will burn longer and hotter, allowing you to add larger pieces of wood to build your fire. The key with kindling, as with tinder, is ensuring it's dry. Look for dead branches on trees or the forest floor that have not been exposed to moisture.

Creativity in finding fire-starting materials can save the day in environments where natural materials are scarce or wet. Certain fungi, like the tinder fungus found on the side of trees, can be used as tinder. Paper, cardboard, or plastic chips can be used as emergency tinder in urban or coastal survival scenarios. However, it's essential to be mindful of the environmental impact.

The process of gathering tinder and kindling is as much about preparation as it is about observation. Developing an eye for spotting potential fire-starting materials as you move through different environments is a skill that improves with practice. Always collect more tinder and kindling than you think you'll need; it's better to have it and not need it than the other way around.

As we transition from the essentials of fire-starting materials and tinder, the next step in our firecraft journey involves building a fire that burns and serves specific purposes, such as heat and cooking. It is crucial to understand the properties of different materials and how they contribute to your fire-making efforts. With the proper preparation and knowledge, creating fire can transform a survival situation, providing warmth, light, and a means to cook food and purify water.

Building a Fire for Heat and Cooking

Having equipped ourselves with the knowledge of gathering suitable materials and tinder, let's delve into the art of building a fire that not only warms but also serves as a reliable cookstove in the wilderness. This skill is fundamental to survival and comfort in the outdoors, transforming a daunting night into a manageable, even cozy, experience.

First and foremost, select a safe location for your fire. It should avoid overhanging branches, dry grass, and other flammable materials. A bare dirt patch is ideal. If the ground is wet or covered in snow, you can create a platform using green logs or stones to insulate your fire from the dampness. Remember, safety is paramount; always consider the direction of the wind to prevent the fire from spreading.

Once you've chosen your spot, it's time to lay the foundation. If you're aiming for heat, a teepee or cone structure is highly effective. Start by placing your tinder bundle in the center, then lean small twigs and kindling around it, forming a cone. This structure allows air to circulate freely, feeding oxygen to the flames and encouraging a robust and steady burn.

For cooking, adaptability is critical. A fire lay that offers stability and adjustable heat is the log cabin build. After igniting your tinder, stack larger sticks around the flames in a square, log cabin style. This method supports your cooking vessel and creates a bed of hot coals that provide consistent, controllable heat.

Lighting the fire is a moment of truth. Ignite your tinder, gently at first, to catch the smaller kindling. As the fire grows, feed it progressively larger pieces of wood, always mindful not to smother the flames. Patience is crucial; a fire rushed is a fire extinguished.

Managing your fire for cooking involves a delicate balance. Initially, you'll want high flames to boil water or cook foods quickly. As the fire matures, it will produce coals. These embers are your best tool for simmering or slow-cooking, offering even heat without the risk of burning your meal. Moving coals closer or further from your pot can adjust the temperature, giving you control over your cooking environment.

Remember, a fire is a living entity in the wilderness. It requires attention and respect to maintain. Keep a supply of wood readily available to feed it as needed, but also be ready to let it die down when it's time to rest. Before retiring or leaving your camp, ensure the fire is completely extinguished. Douse it with water, stir the ashes, and check for warmth. A fire left unattended can quickly become a disaster.

In the next steps of our journey through firecraft, we'll explore how this essential survival tool can also be a beacon of hope and rescue. When done correctly, signaling with fire can guide rescuers to your location, turning a difficult situation into a story of survival and resilience.

Signaling with Fire

The ability to signal for help can mean the difference between life and death. While there are many methods to signal for rescue, using fire is one of the most effective, especially in vast, uninhabited areas. Whilst we've already briefly discussed "Signaling for Help" in Chapter 1, this section delves into the art of signaling with fire, providing practical advice to enhance your chances of being spotted by rescuers.

Firstly, it's crucial to understand the basics of creating a signal fire. Unlike a fire for warmth or cooking, a signal fire must be visible from a great distance. To achieve this, location is vital. Ideally, your signal fire should be positioned on high ground or in a clearing unobstructed by trees or other terrain features. Visibility from the air and the ground should be your primary consideration.

Once you've selected a suitable location, the next step is to prepare the fire. You'll want to create a fire that produces a lot of smoke for signaling purposes. This is achieved using green vegetation or materials that smoke rather than burn quickly. However, before you add these materials, you need to start with a strong, hot base fire. Use dry wood to establish this base, ensuring it's substantial enough to sustain the addition of green materials without being smothered.

Regarding signaling, the traditional method involves creating three fires in a triangle or straight line with about 100 feet (30 meters) between each fire. This arrangement is an internationally recognized distress signal, which can significantly increase your chances of being spotted by rescuers.

If you're in a situation where creating multiple fires

isn't feasible, focus on producing the most smoke from a single fire. Once the base fire is hot and stable, add your green vegetation, rubber (if available), or any other material that produces thick smoke. The goal is to create a contrast against the background, with dark smoke being most visible against a light sky and vice versa.

Timing is also a critical factor in signaling with fire. If you're aware of search efforts or hear aircraft or rescue teams nearby, that's the time to maximize your fire's smoke output. Adding more smoldering materials can draw attention to your location during these periods.

Lastly, safety should never be compromised. Always ensure that your signal fire is manageable and that you have the means to extinguish it if necessary. The last thing you want is a signal fire to turn into a wildfire.

By mastering the skill of signaling with fire, you enhance your survival toolkit, preparing you for the unforeseen. Remember, the goal of wilderness survival is not just to endure but to emerge safely, and effective signaling is a critical component of that goal.

Extinguishing Fires Safely

After mastering the art of signaling with fire, it's equally crucial to understand how to extinguish fires safely and effectively. In the wilderness, managing your fire responsibly ensures your safety and preserving the natural environment around you. Here, we delve into practical techniques and considerations for safely putting out a campfire, a skill every outdoor enthusiast should have in their survival toolkit.

Firstly, planning is key. Always establish your fire in a clear, open space away from overhanging branches, dry grass, and other flammable materials. This precaution minimizes the risk of accidental spread. As your fire serves its purpose, whether for warmth, cooking, or signaling, begin the extinguishing process well before you intend to leave the site or retire for the night.

The most effective and immediate method to extinguish a fire is by using water. Douse your fire with ample water, ensuring that all embers, not just the flames, are thoroughly soaked. The goal is to cool all materials below their ignition point. However, simply throwing water on the fire isn't enough. Stir the ashes and embers with a stick or shovel to expose any hotspots hiding beneath the surface. Continue adding water and stirring until all hissing sounds cease, indicating the fire is out.

If water is scarce, which can often be the case in specific wilderness scenarios, sand or dirt can be an alternative solution. Cover the fire with a generous layer of sand or dirt to smother the flames. Just like with water, mixing and stirring the sand or dirt into the embers is essential to eliminate any hidden pockets of heat. Be cautious, as this method doesn't cool the fire as effectively as water. Ensure the fire is entirely out by feeling above the extinguished area for any heat emanating. If it's too hot to touch, it's too hot to leave.

Another vital aspect of fire extinguishment is timing. Never leave a fire unattended; ensure it's completely extinguished before leaving the site. A good rule of thumb is if it's too hot to touch, it's too hot to leave. This simple check can prevent forest fires and ensure you leave no trace of your presence in the wilderness.

Lastly, consider the environmental impact of your actions. While water and sand are natural elements, excessive use can adversely affect the surrounding ecosystem. Use only as much water as necessary and avoid introducing large amounts of foreign materials like dirt or sand into a water source, which can disrupt aquatic life.

In conclusion, extinguishing fires safely in the wilderness is a fundamental skill that protects you and the environment. By employing these techniques, you ensure that your natural adventures are enjoyable and sustainable, leaving the wilderness as pristine as you found. Remember, a responsible outdoorsperson not only knows how to create fire but also how to extinguish it with care and consideration.

Chapter Summary

- Mastering firecraft is essential for wilderness survival, providing warmth, safety, and comfort.
- Selecting an appropriate site for a fire involves finding a sheltered, well-ventilated area and clearing it of debris.
- Fire requires three elements to thrive: heat, fuel, and oxygen, known as the "fire triangle."
- Gathering materials starts with tinder (easily ignitable materials), followed by kindling (small sticks) to build a flame, and finally, fuel wood (larger pieces) to sustain the fire.

- Assembling the fire typically involves creating a teepee structure with kindling around the tinder, allowing for good air circulation.
- Igniting the tinder can be done with matches, lighter, or primitive techniques, followed by gently blowing to provide oxygen and carefully adding larger pieces of wood.
- For signaling, a fire should be visible from a distance, using materials that produce a lot of smoke and, ideally, creating three fires in a recognizable distress pattern.
- Safely extinguishing a fire involves using water or sand to thoroughly soak or cover it, stirring to expose hotspots, and ensuring it's completely out before leaving.

4

FORAGING FOR FOOD

A group of people forage for food in the wilderness.

Identifying Edible Plants

In wilderness survival, the ability to identify edible plants can be a lifeline. Nature offers a bounty of nourishment, but it requires knowledge and caution to tap into this resource safely. This section delves into the essentials of recognizing plants that can sustain you in the wild.

First and foremost, familiarize yourself with the universal edibility test. This process, while time-consuming, is a valuable tool in determining whether a plant is safe to eat. It involves separating the plant into its essential components—leaves, stems, roots, and so on—and testing each part for edibility by applying a series of steps, including skin contact, tasting a small portion, and waiting for any adverse reactions. Remember, this test is a last resort and should only be used when unsure about a plant's edibility and have no other means of verification.

Knowledge of specific edible plants in the region you are exploring is invaluable. Many areas have unique flora, and what is edible in one place may not be found in another. Invest time in learning about the local vegetation before your adventure. Books, workshops, and guided tours can provide a wealth of information.

Some common edible plants found in various parts of the world include dandelions, whose leaves, flowers, and roots are edible; wild onions and garlic, identifiable by their distinctive smell; and cattails, found near freshwater sources, where the young shoots and roots can be consumed. Berries are also a potential food source, but caution is paramount as some are highly toxic.

Visual identification is crucial. Pay attention to the shape, size, color, and texture of leaves, flowers, and fruits. Many edible plants have poisonous look-alikes, so it's essential to note distinguishing features. For instance, wild carrots (also known as Queen Anne's lace) are edible but closely resemble the poisonous hemlock. The difference lies in the root's smell—wild carrots have a distinct carrot scent, while hemlock roots do not.

Tapping into local knowledge can be a game-changer. Indigenous peoples and local foragers possess generations of knowledge about the land and its resources. If you have the opportunity, learn from them. They can provide insights into which plants are edible and how to prepare them to neutralize toxins and enhance flavor.

In conclusion, foraging for food in the wilderness is both an art and a science. It requires patience, respect for nature, and a commitment to learning. By understanding the basics of plant identification and exercising caution, you can unlock the natural bounty that surrounds you. Remember, the key to successful foraging is knowing what you can eat and recognizing what you must avoid.

Avoiding Poisonous Plants

The bounty of nature offers a plethora of edible plants that can sustain you. But, it's equally important to be aware of the dangers lurking among those beneficial greens. Poisonous plants are not just a minor inconvenience; they can severely threaten your health and survival. This section aims to arm you with the knowledge to navigate the green wilderness safely, ensuring you can distinguish between nourishing sustenance and perilous flora.

First and foremost, familiarize yourself with the universal edibility test. This step-by-step process is a methodical way to determine the safety of a plant when you're unsure of its identity. It involves separating the plant into its essential components—leaves, stems, roots, and so on—and testing them one at a time for adverse reactions. While this test can be a lifesaver, it's time-consuming and should only be used as a last resort.

Knowledge is your best defense against poisonous plants. Before venturing into the wild:

1. Invest time in studying the region's flora.
2. Learn to identify not only the edible plants but also the poisonous ones.
3. Pay attention to details such as the shape of the leaves, the color of the berries, and the texture of the stems.

Books, apps, and local guides can be invaluable resources in this learning process.

Remember, some poisonous plants can mimic their edible counterparts, making them particularly dangerous. For instance, the deadly nightshade berry can easily be mistaken for an edible berry if one is not careful. Always err on caution; if you're unsure about a plant, it's better to leave it alone.

Another crucial tip is to avoid plants with telltale signs of toxicity. These include a bitter or soapy taste, milky or discolored sap, almond scent in woody parts and leaves, grain heads with pink, purplish, or black spurs, and three-leaved growth patterns. While these indicators are not foolproof, they warn that a plant may be harmful.

Lastly, consider the impact of your foraging. Avoid overharvesting and be mindful of the environment. Sustainable foraging ensures that the wilderness thrives and provides for future generations.

By equipping yourself with the knowledge to avoid poisonous plants, you safeguard your health and deepen your connection with nature. As you move on to mastering foraging techniques, remember that respect for the natural world and an understanding of its complexities are the foundations of successful wilderness survival.

Foraging Techniques

Embarking on the journey of foraging in the wilderness is not just about survival; it's about connecting with nature in its most primal form. However, to safely and effectively gather edible plants, nuts, fruits, and mushrooms, one must approach foraging with respect, knowledge, and practical techniques.

First and foremost, understanding the environment you're in is crucial. Different ecosystems offer varying bounties. For example, deciduous forests are rich in nuts and mushrooms, while coastal areas can provide seaweeds and shellfish. Begin your foraging adventure by researching the specific flora of your region.

Equipped with this knowledge, the next step is to familiarize yourself with the seasonal cycles of plants and fungi. Many edible plants have specific seasons when they are abundant, nutritious, and at their peak flavor. Learning these cycles ensures a successful forage and promotes sustainability by allowing plants to regenerate and complete their life cycles.

When you're out in the field, practice the "rule of three" - if you're unsure about the edibility of a plant, leave it. This rule is simple: Do not consume it if you cannot positively identify a plant and confirm it is edible from three separate, reliable sources. This cautious approach is a cornerstone of safe foraging.

Another technique is to start small. When trying a new plant for the first time, even if you're confident in its identification, consume a small amount and wait. Some plants can adversely affect specific individuals, so it's wise to ensure you don't react negatively.

Those looking to forage mushrooms have higher stakes due to the potential for poisonous look-alikes. Invest time in learning from experienced mushroom foragers or join local foraging groups. Many communities offer workshops or guided foraging walks. Remember, with mushrooms, when in doubt, throw it out.

Lastly, ethical foraging is as important as the techniques themselves. Always forage with sustainability in mind. Take only what you need, never deplete a single area of its resources, and be mindful of protected species and habitats. By foraging responsibly, you ensure these natural resources remain abundant for future generations.

As you transition from foraging to other means of wilderness sustenance, remember that the skills and respect for nature you've cultivated will serve you well. Whether gathering wild edibles or setting up traps for small game, sustainability, safety, and respect for the environment should always guide your actions.

Hunting and Trapping Small Game

The ability to secure food from your surroundings is paramount. While foraging for edible plants can sustain you, meat's nutritional value and energy can be a game-changer. This section delves into the essentials of hunting and trapping small game, a skill set that can significantly enhance your survival prospects.

The first step in hunting and trapping is understanding the small game available in your environment. Typical small game includes rabbits, squirrels, birds, and fish, depending on your location. Observing animal tracks, droppings, and feeding areas can give you insights into their habits and the best times to hunt or set traps.

Trapping is often more efficient than hunting, as it allows you to set multiple traps, increasing your chances of capturing game while you attend to other survival tasks. Here are a few simple yet effective traps:

1. **Snare Trap:** A snare is a looped wire or cord that tightens around an animal's neck or limb as it passes through. Position snares on known animal trails or near burrows. Check them regularly to avoid leaving an animal trapped for too long.
2. **Deadfall Trap:** This trap uses a heavy weight, such as a rock or log, which falls and crushes the animal when it disturbs a trigger mechanism. Deadfalls require careful construction and placement to be effective and humane.
3. **Pitfall Trap:** Although more labor-intensive, a pitfall trap involves digging a deep hole to prevent the animal from escaping and covering it lightly with branches and leaves. It's particularly effective for larger rodents.

If trapping isn't an option, or you wish to actively hunt, creating improvised weapons can be your next course of action. A spear can be fashioned from a straight, sturdy stick, sharpened at one end, and hardened over a fire. Slingshots can be made with a Y-shaped branch and elastic material, suitable for small birds and rodents.

Always prioritize ethics and safety when hunting and trapping. Aim to kill quickly and humanely, minimizing suffering. Be aware of local regulations regarding hunting and trapping, and ensure you're not targeting endangered or protected species. Additionally, handle all animals with care to avoid injury and disease transmission.

Mastering the art of hunting and trapping small game can significantly bolster your food resources in a survival situation. By understanding animal behavior, employing simple trapping techniques, and improvising hunting tools, you can secure a vital source of nutrition. Remember, the key is in the capture and, ethically and safely, respecting the wilderness and its inhabitants.

Preparing Wild Food

Transitioning from the skills of hunting and trapping to the art of foraging, we delve into the world of preparing wild food. Foraging offers a sustainable way to supplement your diet with vitamins, minerals, and flavors often absent from the modern diet. However, the

Wilderness Survival Hacks

key to safely enjoying these natural bounties is proper identification, collection, and preparation.

Before you even think about eating a wild plant, identify it positively as edible. Many plants have poisonous look-alikes, so it's crucial to be 100% certain of their identity. Use reliable field guides, and learn from experienced foragers.

When collecting, choose young, tender leaves over older ones, as they are often more palatable and nutritious. Always forage away from polluted areas and roadsides to avoid contaminants. Remember, sustainability is vital: take only what you need and leave enough behind for the plant to thrive.

Once you've gathered your wild edibles, the next step is cleaning. Rinse your foraged goods thoroughly under running water to remove dirt, insects, or other debris. Some plants may require more specific preparation methods to make them safe or more palatable:

- **Boiling:** Certain wild greens, like dandelion leaves, can be bitter. Boiling them in water for a few minutes can help reduce their bitterness. Remember to change the water once or twice during boiling.

- **Soaking**: Some nuts and seeds contain tannins that can be removed by soaking them in water for several hours or overnight. This not only improves their flavor but also their digestibility.
- **Cooking:** Many wild foods, especially root vegetables, are best enjoyed cooked. Cooking not only makes them safer to eat by killing potential pathogens but also makes them easier to digest and their nutrients more accessible.

Incorporating wild foods into your diet doesn't have to be complicated. Here are a couple of simple recipes to get you started:

- **Wild Berry and Nut Mix:** Forage for and wash wild berries, nuts, and edible leaves, ensuring they are safe to eat. Mix them for a nutritious wilderness snack.
- **Fire-Roasted Rabbit with Wild Herbs:** Season a cleaned wild rabbit with salt and freshly foraged herbs like rosemary and thyme, then roast over an open fire until cooked.

While foraging can enrich your diet and connect you with nature, safety should always be your top priority. Only eat something you're 100% sure about, and when trying a new wild food, start with a small amount to see how your body reacts. Remember, the wilderness is not a supermarket; it requires knowledge, respect, and a sense of responsibility.

By mastering the skills of foraging and preparing wild food, you add variety to your wilderness survival diet and deepen your connection with the natural world. The earth can provide abundant nourishment and pleasure with practice, patience, and respect for nature.

Chapter Summary

- Identifying edible plants is crucial for wilderness survival, offering a source of nourishment with knowledge and caution.
- The universal edibility test is a method to determine plant safety for consumption, involving skin contact, tasting, and waiting for reactions.
- Learning about local edible plants through books, workshops, and guided tours is invaluable, as edible flora varies by region.

- Common edible plants include dandelions, wild onions, garlic, cattails, and certain berries. However, caution is advised due to toxic look-alikes.
- Indigenous peoples and local foragers can provide deep insights into edible plants and their preparation to neutralize toxins and enhance flavor.
- Avoiding poisonous plants is critical; familiarize yourself with their characteristics and the universal edibility test to navigate safely.
- Foraging techniques emphasize respect for nature, knowledge of the environment, and ethical practices to ensure sustainability.
- Hunting and trapping small game, alongside foraging for plants, can significantly enhance survival prospects, requiring an understanding of animal behavior and ethical practices.

5
FIRST AID AND HEALTH

A woman and a man in the wilderness performing first aid on a broken leg.

Handling Bites and Stings

In the wilderness, where the beauty of nature meets the unpredictability of the wild, bites and stings can be a common occurrence. Whether it's a curious insect or a hidden snake, knowing how to handle these situations can be the difference between a minor inconvenience and a life-threatening emergency. This section delves into practical and effective methods to manage bites and stings, ensuring your adventure doesn't turn into a misadventure.

Immediate Actions for Insect Bites and Stings

The first step is to remain calm when dealing with insect bites or stings. Panic can accelerate the spread of venom in the body. If the stinger is still present, like bee stings, use a flat-edged object like a credit card to scrape it off. Avoid tweezers or squeezing it out, as this can inject more venom.

After removing the stinger, wash the area with soap and water to prevent infection. Applying a cold pack can reduce swelling and pain. However, ensure a barrier, like a cloth, between the ice and skin to avoid frostbite. For itching, a paste made from baking soda and water can offer relief when applied to the bite site.

Snake Bites

Snake bites, particularly from venomous species,

require immediate and specific actions. The first rule is not to panic or attempt to suck out the venom, a common myth that can do more harm than good. Keep the affected limb immobilized and lower than the heart to slow venom spread. Do not apply a tourniquet or ice, which can cause further tissue damage.

Seeking professional medical help is crucial, even if unsure about the snake's venomous nature. While waiting for help, remove any jewelry or tight clothing near the bite area to allow for swelling. Remember, the goal is to keep the victim calm and still, reducing the heart rate and slowing the venom's spread.

Ticks

Ticks are masters of going unnoticed, making them particularly dangerous as they can transmit diseases. If you find a tick attached to your skin, use fine-tipped tweezers to grasp it as close to the skin's surface as possible. Pull upward with steady, even pressure. After removal, clean the bite area and your hands with rubbing alcohol, soap, and water.

Monitor the bite site for several weeks for any signs of rash or infection. Consult a healthcare provider immediately if you develop symptoms like fever, chills, or muscle aches.

Spiders

For spider bites, identification is critical. While most spider bites are harmless, those from a black widow or brown recluse spider require immediate medical attention. Symptoms of a dangerous spider bite can include severe pain, abdominal cramping, or a significant wound from tissue damage. If you suspect a bite from one of these spiders, apply ice to reduce swelling and seek medical help.

Prevention: Your Best Defense

While knowing how to handle bites and stings is essential, prevention remains the best strategy. Wear protective clothing, use insect repellent, and stay vigilant in environments where bites and stings are common. At night, use bed nets if sleeping in an exposed area. Always check your gear, clothing, and bedding for unwanted guests.

In conclusion, while the wilderness offers unparalleled experiences, it has risks. By understanding how to handle bites and stings effectively, you can ensure that your outdoor adventures remain safe and enjoyable. Remember, the key is preparation, calmness, and swift action.

Natural Remedies

Did you know that nature can often provide its pharmacy in the wilderness? Understanding how to harness these natural remedies can be vital in managing health issues when you're far from conventional medical help. This section delves into natural remedies, offering practical advice on using the resources around you to maintain health and treat common ailments.

One of the most versatile plants you might encounter is the aloe vera. Known for its soothing properties, aloe vera gel can be applied to burns, cuts, and skin irritations, providing relief and promoting healing. If you have a sunburn or a minor kitchen burn while camping, look for an aloe plant, slice open a leaf, and apply the gel directly to the affected area.

Another invaluable natural remedy is activated charcoal from burnt wood or plant material. It's known for absorbing toxins, making it a valuable treatment for certain types of poisoning or stomach issues. If someone ingests a harmful substance, administering activated charcoal can help bind the toxin and prevent absorption by the body. However, it's crucial to seek professional medical advice as soon as possible in cases of poisoning.

For those dealing with insect bites or stings,

plantain leaves, not to be confused with the banana-like fruit, can be a quick fix. These common weeds, often found in disturbed soils, have anti-inflammatory and wound-healing properties. Crushing and applying the leaves directly to the bite or sting can reduce pain and swelling.

Willow bark is another natural remedy with a long history of use. It contains salicin, a compound similar to aspirin, and can relieve pain, fever, and inflammation. You can chew on the raw bark or brew a tea to utilize willow bark. However, it's essential to correctly identify the willow tree and note that people allergic to aspirin should avoid using willow bark.

Lastly, for those navigating through stress or sleeplessness under the stars, consider the calming effects of chamomile. If you have chamomile tea bags, brewing a cup in the evening can help soothe nerves and promote a restful sleep. Chamomile flowers grow wild in many parts of the world. Still, it's essential to positively identify the plant before using it for tea to avoid consuming something potentially harmful.

While these natural remedies can relieve minor ailments and discomforts, they are not substitutes for professional medical treatment. Always prioritize safety and seek medical attention for serious injuries or conditions. However, utilizing these natural resources can enhance your self-reliance and comfort during your wilderness adventures.

Preventing and Treating Hypothermia and Heatstroke

Knowing how to prevent and treat hypothermia and heatstroke can distinguish between a memorable adventure and a life-threatening ordeal. These conditions represent the body's struggle to maintain its core temperature, battling the cold or the heat. Understanding the signs and knowing the immediate steps to take can save lives.

Hypothermia occurs when the body loses heat faster than it can produce it, causing the core body temperature to drop below 95°F (35°C). It can happen in temperatures as mild as 50°F (10°C) if a person is wet and exposed to wind. Prevention starts with layering clothing, focusing on materials that retain warmth even when wet, such as wool or synthetic fibers. Always keep the head and extremities covered, as a significant amount of body heat is lost through the head, hands, and feet.

Should you or a companion begin to show signs of hypothermia—shivering, slurred speech, clumsiness, confusion, or fatigue—it's crucial to act quickly. Move the person to shelter if possible. Replace any wet clothing with dry, warm layers. Share body heat by huddling close; if you have a sleeping bag, use it to trap warmth. Warm, sweet beverages can help increase the body's temperature, but avoid alcohol and caffeine, which can worsen the condition.

Conversely, heatstroke results from the body overheating, typically in temperatures above 90°F (32°C). It can occur due to prolonged exposure to high temperatures or physical exertion in hot weather. Prevention involves:

- Staying hydrated.
- Wearing light-colored and loose-fitting clothing.
- Avoiding strenuous activity during the hottest parts of the day.

Always be aware of the signs of heat exhaustion, which can precede heatstroke: heavy sweating, weakness, cold, pale and clammy skin, nausea, or vomiting.

If someone shows signs of heatstroke—high body temperature, hot and possibly dry skin, rapid pulse, headache, dizziness, nausea, confusion, or unconsciousness—immediate cooling is necessary.

Move the person to a cooler place, remove excess clothing, and cool them down with whatever means available: a cool bath, wet cloths, or fanning. Hydration is critical, but only if the person is conscious and can swallow; give them water or sports drinks to sip slowly.

In both scenarios, monitoring the person closely and seeking medical attention as soon as possible is vital. While these first aid measures can stabilize and improve the situation, professional medical help is essential to address these severe conditions fully.

Understanding these principles prepares you for the challenges of the wilderness. It equips you with the knowledge to help others in need. Remember, the wilderness demands respect, and part of that respect involves preparation and awareness of the risks, including the dangers posed by extreme temperatures.

Mental Health and Coping Mechanisms

It's easy to overlook the crucial aspect of mental health. Yet, maintaining mental and emotional well-being is as vital as addressing physical injuries or environmental threats like hypothermia and heatstroke. This section delves into practical coping mechanisms and strategies to ensure your mental resilience matches your physical endurance when facing the unpredictability of the wild.

The first step in managing your mental health in a survival situation is recognizing the body's natural stress responses: fight, flight, or freeze. These reactions are your body's way of preparing to face a threat. However, in a prolonged survival situation, these responses can become your biggest adversaries if not correctly managed. Recognizing the signs of stress in yourself—such as increased heart rate, rapid breathing, and difficulty focusing—can help you take early steps to mitigate their impact.

One of the most effective ways to control stress and anxiety in the wilderness is through controlled breathing techniques. For instance, the "4-7-8" technique involves breathing in for 4 seconds, holding the breath for 7 seconds, and exhaling slowly for 8 seconds. This method helps reduce anxiety and can bring your focus back to the present, making tackling the task at hand easier.

In a survival situation, it's easy to become overwhelmed by what you're facing. To maintain mental clarity and a sense of progress, break down your survival tasks into small, manageable goals. Whether it's building a shelter, finding water, or simply making it through the next hour, focusing on one task at a time can help keep feelings of despair at bay and provide a sense of accomplishment.

Establishing a routine can provide a sense of normalcy and control in an otherwise unpredictable environment. Simple tasks, like setting up and breaking down camp at the exact times each day, can offer comfort and a sense of order. This routine can also ensure that essential tasks are noticed in the stress of the moment.

Maintaining a positive outlook is crucial for mental endurance. This doesn't mean ignoring the reality of your situation but rather focusing on what you can control and finding reasons to be hopeful. Celebrate your successes, no matter how small, and remind yourself of your strengths and capabilities.

If you're not alone, lean on the social support available. Sharing feelings, offering encouragement, and working together towards common goals can significantly boost morale and reduce the psychological burden of survival.

Engaging in mental exercises like visualization, meditation, or even simple games can distract you from stressors and improve your mood. Visualization can be compelling; imagining a successful outcome or recalling a happy memory can provide a mental escape and renew your determination.

Surviving in the wilderness requires a holistic approach that includes physical survival skills and strategies for maintaining mental health. Understanding and managing stress responses, employing practical coping mechanisms, and fostering a positive, goal-oriented mindset can significantly improve your resilience in adversity. Remember, the wilderness may test you, but it can also reveal untapped wells of mental and emotional strength.

Chapter Summary

- Encounters with wildlife and insects in the wilderness can lead to bites and stings, some of which may be serious if not treated properly.
- For insect stings, it's essential to remove the stinger quickly without squeezing it, clean the area, and apply ice to reduce swelling.
- Snake bites should not be treated with myths like sucking out venom; instead, immobilize the limb and seek medical help immediately.
- Spider bites from dangerous species like black widows or brown recluses require immediate medical attention for symptoms like severe pain or tissue damage.

- To remove tick bites, use fine-tipped tweezers, clean the area, and monitor for signs of diseases like Lyme disease.
- Prevention of bites and stings includes wearing protective clothing, using insect repellent, and staying vigilant in risky environments.
- Natural remedies in the wilderness include aloe vera for burns, activated charcoal for poisoning, and plantain leaves for insect bites.
- Managing mental health in the wilderness involves recognizing stress responses, employing breathing techniques, setting small goals, maintaining a routine, staying positive, seeking social support, and engaging in mental exercises.

6
SURVIVAL GEAR ESSENTIALS

A backpacker holding a compass.

The Survival Kit

In wilderness survival, your kit is not just a collection of items but your lifeline. It's essential to understand that the effectiveness of your survival kit hinges not just on what you include but on how well each tool serves its purpose. This brings us to a critical aspect of wilderness preparedness: choosing the right tools for your survival kit.

The cornerstone of selecting the right tools lies in understanding the environment you're venturing into and the challenges you might face. A desert explorer's kit will differ vastly from that of a mountaineer or a jungle trekker. However, specific tools have universal utility, regardless of the terrain.

Firstly, a high-quality, multi-purpose knife is indispensable. It serves numerous survival needs, from preparing food to crafting shelter. The choice between a fixed blade and a folding knife often comes down to personal preference and the specific demands of your adventure. Fixed blades are generally more durable and reliable for heavy-duty tasks while folding knives offer convenience and portability.

Next, a reliable fire starter is crucial. Options range from waterproof matches and lighters to magnesium fire starters and ferro rods. Each has advantages, but having at least two different types in your kit can prepare you for varying conditions. Remember, the ability to start a fire can mean the difference between life and death in the wilderness, providing warmth, light, and a means to cook food and purify water.

Navigation tools are also vital. While technology has given us GPS devices and smartphones, these can fail or run out of power. A traditional compass and waterproof map of the area you're exploring should always be part of your kit. Understanding how to use these tools effectively before you embark on your journey is just as important as having them.

Water purification methods are another critical component. Whether you opt for purification tablets, a portable filter, or a UV light purifier, ensure you can make natural water sources safe to drink. Dehydration can quickly become a severe threat to survival, making water purification a top priority.

Lastly, a first aid kit tailored to your specific needs and the nature of your adventure should always be noticed. Include personal medications, bandages, antiseptic wipes, and other needed items in an emergency. The contents of your first aid kit should reflect the activities you're undertaking and the potential injuries you might encounter.

Choosing the right tools for your survival kit is about balancing the need for versatility, reliability, and weight. Each item should serve multiple purposes and be tested and familiar to you before setting out.

Remember, your survival kit is your best friend in the wilderness – choose its contents wisely.

Choosing the Right Tools

The gear you carry can mean the difference between a manageable and dire situation. After understanding the basics of what constitutes a comprehensive survival kit, the next crucial step is discerning which tools are essential for your specific needs and how to select them wisely. This section delves into choosing the right tools for your wilderness adventures, ensuring you're well-equipped for whatever nature throws your way.

First and foremost, prioritize multi-purpose tools. Space and weight are at a premium in any pack, and each item you carry should serve multiple functions. A classic example is a Swiss Army knife or a multi-tool, which combines several tools in one compact package. Look for items that can fulfill multiple purposes, such as a hatchet that can be used for chopping wood and hammering.

Durability is another crucial factor. Your survival gear should be able to withstand the rigors of the outdoors. This means opting for items made from high-quality materials that are known for their strength and longevity. Stainless steel tools, for example, resist rust and endure harsh conditions, making them a wise choice for any survival kit.

Consider the environment you'll be venturing into as well. Different terrains and climates require different tools. For instance, a water purifier is indispensable in areas with uncertain access to clean water. At the same time, a sturdy pair of snowshoes is essential for traversing snowy landscapes. Tailor your gear to the specific challenges and resources of the environment you'll be exploring.

Ease of use is another critical consideration. In a survival situation, you want tools that are straightforward and reliable. Complex gadgets may seem appealing, but in high-stress scenarios, simplicity often prevails. Choose tools that you can operate efficiently, even under pressure.

Lastly, educate yourself on the use of each tool in your kit. Owning a high-quality survival tool is only beneficial if you know how to use it effectively. Take the time to practice and become proficient with each piece of equipment before you find yourself in a survival situation.

As we transition from understanding the foundational elements of a survival kit to exploring the possibilities of creating your gear, remember that the tools you carry are as much about personal preference as practicality. The right tools for you are those that align with your skills, your environment, and your survival strategy. With careful selection and a bit of know-how, you can assemble a kit that not only enhances your wilderness experience but could also save your life.

DIY Survival Gear

Having the right gear can mean the difference between a minor inconvenience and a life-threatening situation. However, only some have the budget or access to high-end survival gear. This is where ingenuity and some DIY skills come in handy. By creating your own survival gear, you save money and gain a deeper understanding of how each piece functions, which can be invaluable in a survival scenario.

One of the most versatile and essential pieces of survival gear is a multi-purpose tool. While commercial versions are available, you can create a basic version using items you likely already have at home. Start with a sturdy pocketknife, the cornerstone of your DIY multi-tool. You can add a mini flashlight, a small fire starter kit (which can be as simple as a few matches and a striker), and a compact signal mirror. These items can be bundled with a strong rubber band or encased in a handmade pouch. The key is to ensure that your DIY multi-tool is compact enough to carry easily but comprehensive enough to be useful in various survival situations.

Another critical piece of survival gear is a water filtration system. Clean drinking water is paramount, and while boiling water is an effective method to purify it, having a portable filtration system can be a lifesaver. A simple DIY water filter can be made using a small plastic bottle, cotton cloth, charcoal, sand, and gravel. By layering these materials in the bottle, you create a basic but effective filtration system that can remove particulates and improve the taste of water from natural sources.

Shelter is another vital aspect of wilderness survival. While nothing can entirely replace a high-quality tent, there are ways to improvise in an emergency. One of the most straightforward DIY shelters is a tarp shelter. With a durable tarp, some paracord, and a little know-how, you can create a variety of shelters to protect yourself from the elements. The key to a successful tarp shelter is choosing the right location and ensuring it is securely anchored. This can be achieved by tying your paracord to trees or using rocks and logs to weigh down the tarp's edges.

Lastly, always appreciate the importance of an

excellent first aid kit. While many items in a commercial kit can be purchased individually, you can supplement it with DIY alternatives. For example, duct tape can be used in place of medical tape for securing bandages, and a clean cotton shirt can be torn into strips for use as gauze. Additionally, familiarizing yourself with natural remedies and medicinal plants can enhance your DIY first aid kit and provide you with more options in a wilderness survival situation.

Creating your survival gear equips you with the tools you need to face the wilderness and instills confidence and self-reliance. Remember, the goal of DIY survival gear is not to replace high-quality commercial equipment but to complement it and provide alternatives when necessary. As you become more proficient in crafting your gear, you'll find that your ability to adapt and overcome in the wilderness will grow exponentially.

Maintaining Your Gear

Your gear is not just a set of tools—it's your lifeline. Thus, maintaining your survival gear is as crucial as having it in the first place. This section delves into practical strategies to ensure your equipment remains in top condition, ready to serve its purpose when you need it most.

Firstly, regular inspection of your gear is non-negotiable. Before and after each wilderness excursion, take the time to check each item thoroughly for signs of wear and tear. Look for damage that could compromise the item's functionality, such as cracks in water containers, fraying on rope ends or dullness in knife blades. Early detection of potential issues allows for timely repairs or replacements, preventing equipment failure in critical moments.

Cleaning your gear is equally important. Dirt, grime, and moisture can degrade materials, reducing their effectiveness and lifespan. After every use, clean your tools according to the manufacturer's instructions. For example, wash and dry metal items to prevent rust, air out sleeping bags and tents to avoid mildew, and clean filters in water purification devices to ensure optimal performance.

Proper storage is another critical aspect of gear maintenance. Store your equipment in a cool, dry place away from direct sunlight and extreme temperatures, which can cause materials to deteriorate. Keep sharp objects safely sheathed and place electronics in waterproof containers to protect them from moisture. Organizing your gear thoughtfully also means you can access it quickly when preparing for your next adventure.

Repairing your gear is a skill that every wilderness enthusiast should cultivate. Familiarize yourself with basic repair techniques, such as patching holes in fabric, fixing broken buckles, and sharpening blades. A well-stocked repair kit, including items like duct tape, sewing materials, and multi-purpose glue, can be a game-changer in extending the life of your gear.

Lastly, upgrading your gear is an ongoing process. While maintaining your equipment can significantly extend its usability, there comes a time when replacement or upgrade becomes necessary. Stay informed about advancements in survival gear technology and consider how new items could enhance your wilderness experience. However, always weigh the benefits of new gear against the familiarity and reliability of your existing equipment.

In conclusion, maintaining your survival gear requires a proactive approach, encompassing regular inspection, cleaning, proper storage, repair, and thoughtful upgrading. By dedicating time and effort to care for your equipment, you ensure that it remains reliable, functional, and ready to support you in your wilderness adventures. Remember, the condition of your gear can make the difference between thriving and merely surviving in the great outdoors.

Innovative Uses for Common Items

As we delve into wilderness survival, we must recognize that the most ordinary items can transform into indispensable tools under dire circumstances. This section explores the innovative uses for standard items, turning everyday objects into survival gear essentials.

Dental Floss: Beyond its primary dental hygiene use, it is solid and versatile. It can be used as a fishing line, a snare for small game, or to tie together shelter materials. Its compact size and lightweight nature make it an unassuming yet valuable addition to any survival kit.

Aluminum Foil: Often overlooked, aluminum foil is a multifaceted tool in survival situations. It can be molded into a container to boil water, used as a reflective signal for rescue, or fashioned into a makeshift fishing lure. Wrapping it around your body or shelter can help retain heat during cold nights.

Sanitary Pads: While it might seem unconventional, sanitary pads are highly absorbent and sterile, making them excellent for first aid purposes, such as dressing wounds. They can also be used as fire starters; the cotton material catches fire quickly, especially when separated into thinner layers.

Plastic Bags: These ubiquitous items can serve multiple purposes in the wilderness. A clear plastic bag can be used for solar water disinfection (SODIS), where the sun's UV rays purify water. Plastic bags can also collect rainwater or as a waterproofing layer for keeping essential items dry.

Condoms: Despite their intended use, condoms have properties that make them surprisingly useful for survival. They can hold a significant amount of water, making them useful for storage. They are also stretchable and can be used as makeshift rubber bands for securing or bundling items.

Chapstick: Beyond moisturizing lips, Chapstick can be a valuable tool in survival scenarios. The wax can be used to waterproof small items or to lubricate zippers and other gear. Combined with a cotton ball, it can also serve as a productive fire starter.

Eyeglasses: If you wear eyeglasses, they can be more than just a vision aid. In sunny conditions, the lenses can focus sunlight to start a fire. This method requires patience and precision but can be a lifesaver when matches or lighters are unavailable.

Steel Wool: Commonly used for cleaning, steel wool can also be a vital survival tool. When touched by the terminals of a battery, it can ignite and serve as a fire starter. This is particularly useful in damp conditions where traditional methods may fail.

By reimagining the uses of these everyday items, you can significantly enhance your survival toolkit without adding bulk or excessive weight. This approach prepares you for unexpected situations and encourages creativity and resourcefulness in the wilderness. Remember, the most ordinary items can become extraordinary tools in survival scenarios.

Chapter Summary

- Understanding the environment and challenges ahead is crucial for selecting the right tools for a survival kit, with some tools having universal utility.
- A high-quality, multi-purpose knife and a reliable fire starter are indispensable in any survival kit for tasks like preparing food and starting fires.
- Navigation tools, such as a traditional compass and waterproof map, are vital, especially when technology fails.

- Water purification methods are essential to make natural water sources safe to drink, highlighting the importance of hydration in survival situations.
- A tailored first aid kit should address specific needs and potential injuries, including personal medications and emergency items.
- The selection of survival gear should prioritize multi-purpose tools, durability, and suitability for the specific environment and challenges.
- DIY survival gear, like an essential multi-tool or a simple water filtration system, can be a cost-effective and educational approach to preparedness.
- Regular inspection, cleaning, proper storage, repair, and thoughtful gear upgrading are essential for maintaining survival equipment.

7

WATER CROSSINGS AND TRAVEL

A dangerous river crossing.

Crossing Rivers Safely

Crossing rivers in the wilderness demands a careful approach, combining caution, knowledge, and sometimes courage. The decision on how and whether to cross is crucial for safety. Here are vital tips and techniques for safely navigating this aspect of wilderness travel.

Before attempting to cross, thoroughly assess the river, considering its width, depth, and current speed. Swollen rivers from recent rains or snowmelt may necessitate waiting or finding another route, as water above knee height can sweep you off your feet, and fast-moving water poses a danger even if shallow.

Choosing the right spot to cross is essential. Look for a straight section of the river where you can consistently assess flow and depth, avoiding bends where the outer side is often more profound and faster. Areas where the river widens, indicating shallower and slower water or places with visible rocks or sandbars are preferable for crossing.

Preparation involves loosening backpack straps for easy removal if you fall while keeping it on for potential buoyancy. Secure loose items and waterproof essential gear. Use a sturdy stick or trekking pole for stability and to probe the water ahead.

When crossing, face upstream, leaning into the current to maintain balance, and move sideways with small, shuffling steps, keeping your feet on the riverbed. Avoid crossing directly or downstream to reduce slipping or being pushed over risks. If in a group, crossing together can offer additional stability.

Recognizing when a river is too dangerous to cross is crucial. If in doubt, it's safer to turn back or wait for conditions to improve, prioritizing safety over progress.

Adhering to these guidelines enhances the likelihood of a safe river crossing. However, each river and situation is unique, necessitating judgment and opting for the safest choice when uncertain. Successfully crossing a river may lead to further challenges, such as building rafts or floats for larger bodies of water or impassable obstacles, requiring adaptation and different survival skills.

Building Rafts and Floats

The ability to traverse water bodies safely and effectively can be a matter of survival in the wilderness. After understanding the principles of crossing rivers safely, it's equally crucial to grasp the basics of constructing rafts and floats, especially when swimming or wading isn't viable due to the water's depth, current strength, or temperature.

Building a raft or float requires ingenuity and understanding basic buoyancy principles. The first step is to scout for materials that can float. Deadwood, dried reeds, and bundles of lighter branches are excellent starting points. In some environments, you may also find buoyant materials like empty plastic bottles or foam pieces, which can be repurposed effectively.

The construction of a raft hinges on creating a stable platform. Begin by laying out two longer logs parallel to each other, which will serve as the base of your raft. These should be thick enough to support your weight and the weight of any gear you need to transport. Across these, tie shorter logs or branches to form the raft's deck. Use vines, strips of bark, or even sturdy grasses as rope, ensuring each piece is securely fastened to prevent your raft from coming apart mid-crossing.

For floats, the approach is slightly different. If you're in a pinch, tying a bundle of light branches or reeds together can create a makeshift floatation device. This won't offer a raft's stability or carrying capacity but can be a quick solution to keep you buoyant. Similarly, if you've managed to find or salvage plastic bottles, securing them together in a net or with rope can create an effective float. This method is beneficial for supporting your weight while swimming across a body of water.

Testing is a critical next step before committing to your crossing. Place your raft or float into the water near the shore and gradually apply weight to assess its buoyancy and stability. It's better to discover any weaknesses while you're still within easy reach of land.

Remember, the goal of using a raft or float is not speed but safety. Once you're on the water, maintain a low center of gravity to avoid capsizing. Use a long stick or branch as a makeshift paddle to help guide your raft or assist in swimming with your float.

In constructing these survival aids, creativity and resourcefulness are your best tools. Each situation may call for a different approach based on the materials at hand and the specific challenges of the water body you're facing. With practice and patience, building rafts and floats can become a valuable skill in your wilderness survival toolkit, bridging the gap between the shores of uncertainty and the land of safety.

Swimming in Open Water

Swimming in open water can be daunting, especially when you are in a wilderness survival situation. However, you can navigate these waters safely and efficiently with the proper knowledge and techniques. This section will guide you through the essential tips and strategies for swimming in open water, ensuring you're prepared for whatever challenges you face.

First and foremost, it's crucial to assess the water conditions before diving in. Look for currents, obstacles, and any signs of wildlife that could pose a threat. If the water is running fast, consider looking for a narrower section where the speed might decrease, or use natural barriers to your advantage to cross safely.

When it comes to swimming technique, conserving energy is critical. Use a relaxed, steady stroke to maintain a consistent pace without exhausting yourself. The breaststroke and sidestroke are particularly effective for this purpose, as they provide good buoyancy and visibility. Keep your movements as smooth and flat as possible to reduce drag and make swimming easier.

Buoyancy aids can be a lifesaver in open water. If you're crossing a long distance, having something that helps you float can conserve energy and provide a sense of security. If available, this could be a life jacket or improvised flotation devices made from materials at hand, such as sealed plastic bags filled with air or foam pieces.

Navigation is another critical aspect of swimming in open water. Always have a clear destination and use landmarks to guide your way. Use the sun or stars to maintain your direction if visibility is low. Swimming parallel to the shore is also wise when possible, providing a reference point and a quick escape route if needed.

Lastly, always appreciate the importance of staying calm. Panic is your worst enemy in survival situations, especially in open water. Maintain a positive mindset, focus on breathing, and keep a steady pace. Remember, your mental resilience is just as important as your physical endurance.

By following these guidelines, you can navigate open waters with confidence. Remember, preparation and knowledge are your best tools for wilderness survival. Stay informed, stay calm, and you'll be well-equipped to handle whatever comes your way.

Dealing with Marine Hazards

Navigating through wilderness water bodies requires a keen understanding of marine environments' challenges and potential hazards. Dealing with these hazards effectively ensures safety and success in wilderness survival. This includes practical strategies and tips for handling situations during water crossings and travel.

When crossing rivers, streams, or coastal areas, one of the most significant risks comes from the force of moving water. Currents can be surprisingly strong, and tides can quickly change the depth and intensity of water bodies. To safely navigate these, it's essential to assess the water from the shore before attempting to cross, looking for signs of solid currents or a noticeable pull. Planning your crossing during low tide can make the water calmer and shallower for tides. If caught in a strong current, swimming parallel to the shore until you can escape the current's pull and then angling back towards the shore is advised.

Submerged logs, rocks, and vegetation are severe threats to travelers, potentially trapping or injuring you. Since clear visibility is rare in wilderness settings, moving cautiously and using a stick or pole to probe the water ahead can help identify obstacles. It's crucial to move slowly and ensure a firm footing before advancing.

Encounters with marine life, ranging from leeches in freshwater to jellyfish in saltwater, can vary from being nuisances to posing severe dangers. Wearing clothing or a wet suit to cover as much skin as possible in areas known for harmful marine life can minimize risks. In areas with jellyfish, dragging a stick through the water ahead of you can help deter them. Seeking first aid immediately after encountering potentially harmful marine life is essential for addressing any injuries or adverse reactions.

Hypothermia is a risk even in warm climates,

especially during crossings in cold rivers or lakes. Keeping crossings brief and having dry clothes ready to change immediately afterward can protect against hypothermia. If crossing in a group, doing so together can provide additional warmth and stability against currents.

Water quality is another concern, as polluted or stagnant water can harbor bacteria and parasites harmful to humans. It's important to avoid ingesting water during crossings and to clean any part of your body that comes into contact with suspicious water as soon as possible.

Being prepared and knowledgeable about these marine hazards can significantly reduce the risks associated with water crossings and travel in the wilderness. Caution, preparation, and respect for the power of nature are vital principles for successful navigation, setting you on the path to mastering safe and efficient water crossings.

Conserving Energy During Travel

Mastering the art of energy conservation during travel, especially after navigating through marine hazards, is crucial. The transition from water crossings to continued travel on land demands a strategic approach to preserve your strength and resources. Here, we delve into practical hacks to conserve energy, ensuring you remain robust and ready to face the challenges ahead.

Firstly, it's essential to understand the principle of pacing. Unlike a sprint, survival is a marathon. After dealing with the unpredictability of water, your body needs to recover even as you move. Adopt a pace that allows you to breathe easily and speak in complete sentences. This pace might seem slow, but it's sustainable, ensuring you can cover more ground without overexerting yourself.

Secondly, the importance of planning must be balanced. Before embarking on the next leg of your journey, take a moment to assess your route. Look for paths that offer the least resistance. Dense underbrush, steep inclines, and rocky terrains are energy zappers. Whenever possible, choose flat, clear paths. Utilize natural landmarks to navigate, reducing the need for constant map checks or GPS usage, which can mentally drain you.

Hydration and nutrition play pivotal roles in energy conservation. Your body functions best when adequately fueled. After a water crossing, replenish any lost fluids and electrolytes. Snack on high-energy, nutrient-dense foods that are easy to digest. Foods like nuts, dried fruits, and energy bars offer a quick energy boost without the sluggishness of heavier meals.

Another hack lies in the art of layering your clothing. Conditions can change rapidly, and managing your body temperature is critical to conserving energy. Wet clothes can lead to hypothermia, even in mild conditions, draining your energy reserves. Change into dry clothes if available, or wring out wet garments to remove excess water. Dress in layers that can be easily adjusted to prevent overheating or chilling.

Lastly, rest is as important as movement. Short, strategic breaks can significantly boost your endurance. Find a comfortable spot to sit or lie down, elevate your feet to reduce swelling, and take deep breaths to lower your heart rate. Even a 10-minute rest can rejuvenate your body and mind, making the next stretch of your journey more manageable.

In conclusion, transitioning from water crossings to land travel in a survival situation requires a mindful approach to energy conservation. You can significantly enhance your endurance and overall survival by pacing yourself, planning your route, managing your nutrition and hydration, dressing appropriately, and incorporating rest. Remember, in the wilderness, wise energy use is just as important as the distance you cover.

Chapter Summary

- Crossing rivers safely involves assessing the river's width, depth, and current speed and sometimes waiting for conditions to improve or finding an alternative route.
- Ideal crossing points are straight river sections, avoiding bends and looking for shallower, slower areas with visible rocks or sandbars for support.
- Preparation for crossing includes loosening backpack straps for quick release if needed, securing loose items, and using a stick or trekking pole for stability.
- Proper crossing involves facing upstream, leaning into the current, and moving sideways with small shuffling steps, with group crossings offering added stability.
- Knowing when to turn back is crucial, prioritizing safety over progress if the river seems too dangerous.
- Building rafts and floats from materials like deadwood, dried reeds, or plastic bottles can aid in crossing deeper or stronger currents,

with stability and buoyancy testing essential before use.
- Swimming in open water requires assessing conditions, using energy-conserving strokes like breaststroke or sidestroke, utilizing buoyancy aids, navigating with landmarks or celestial bodies, and staying calm.
- Dealing with marine hazards includes understanding how to navigate currents and tides, avoiding underwater obstacles, protecting against harmful marine life, preventing hypothermia, and ensuring water quality, with energy conservation strategies like pacing, route planning, proper nutrition and hydration, layering clothing, and resting effectively for continued travel on land.

8
WEATHER AND ENVIRONMENT

Rainy weather in the wilderness.

Predicting Weather Patterns

Understanding and predicting weather patterns becomes a crucial survival skill in the heart of the wilderness.

The ability to read the sky, the behavior of animals, and the patterns of nature can mean the difference between being prepared for a sudden storm and being caught off guard. This section delves into traditional and modern methods to forecast weather, ensuring you can adapt to your environment effectively.

One of the most accessible indicators of impending weather changes is the sky. Cloud formations, in particular, can tell us much about what to expect. For instance, high, wispy cirrus clouds often indicate fair weather. Still, their gradual accumulation can suggest a change is on the horizon, usually indicating that a storm system may be moving in. With their towering presence, Cumulonimbus clouds are a clear signal of thunderstorms and potentially severe weather. Identifying these and other cloud types can give you a heads-up hours or days in advance.

Another traditional method of predicting weather involves observing animal behavior. Many animals are susceptible to changes in air pressure and can behave differently as weather systems approach. Birds flying lower than usual can indicate bad weather ahead, as they try to avoid the discomfort of flying in lower pressures that precede storms. Frogs are known to croak louder and more frequently when bad weather is on the way, a survival instinct tied to their breeding patterns.

Wilderness Survival Hacks

The behavior of plants can also offer clues about the weather. For example, some flowers close their petals in anticipation of rain. Pine cones open up in dry weather and close in moist weather due to the expansion and contraction of their scales in response to humidity.

In addition to these natural indicators, modern technology has given us tools that can aid in weather prediction. Portable weather radios provide updates and warnings, invaluable in areas prone to sudden weather changes. Smartphone apps can offer real-time weather data and forecasts. However, it's important to remember that you may only sometimes have a signal in remote wilderness areas.

Understanding these signs and signals requires patience and practice. It's a skill to develop over time through observation and experience. By paying attention to the sky, wildlife, and plant life and using available technology, you can become adept at predicting weather patterns. This knowledge enriches your outdoor experience and enhances your ability to stay safe in the wilderness.

As we move forward, it's crucial to remember that predicting the weather is just one aspect of dealing with environmental challenges. The next step is learning how to survive and thrive in the extreme conditions that nature can throw our way. Your ability to adapt and utilize survival strategies will be tested, whether in extreme heat or cold.

Surviving in Extreme Conditions

Conditions can quickly change from safe to dangerous, requiring physical strength, environmental knowledge, and quick adaptation. This discussion focuses on essential survival techniques that could mean the difference between life and death in nature's extreme situations.

Finding or creating shelter is a top priority in harsh conditions. The shelter provides necessary shade in intense heat, while in cold environments, it offers warmth and protection from the wind. While natural shelters like caves can be lifesavers, often you'll need to build your own. In snowy conditions, igloos or snow caves can keep you warm and block the wind, and in forests, lean-tos constructed from branches and leaves can protect you from rain and sun. The goal is to utilize what the environment offers to make your shelter as sturdy and insulated as possible.

Dealing with extreme heat involves managing the risk of dehydration and heatstroke. It's vital to find and purify water, with boiling being the most reliable method. However, solar stills can work in dry areas.

Wearing loose, light-colored clothing helps prevent heatstroke, and it's essential to stay shaded and cover your head and neck during peak sun hours.

In cold settings, staying hydrated is equally challenging, and it's safer to melt snow or ice before consuming to avoid lowering your body temperature. Avoiding alcohol and caffeine is wise, as they can dehydrate you. Staying warm involves layering clothes, staying dry, recognizing signs of hypothermia and frostbite, ensuring extremities are protected, and avoiding tight clothing that restricts blood flow.

Finding food becomes crucial in extreme conditions as your body needs more energy. Knowing local flora and fauna can transform a seemingly barren area into a food source. Fish and game can be plentiful in colder climates, but you must know how to trap or fish. Knowing which plants are edible and how to forage in warmer climates efficiently can save your life.

Navigating through extreme terrains requires careful planning and energy conservation. Knowing how to make and use snowshoes or safely traverse glaciers is essential in snowy or icy conditions. Using the sun, stars, or natural landmarks in deserts or jungles can prevent getting lost in vast, featureless areas.

Surviving in extreme conditions is as much a mental challenge as a physical one. Overcoming fear, loneliness, and uncertainty is crucial. Keeping a positive attitude, setting achievable goals, and staying busy can help combat despair. Survival is more than just enduring; it's about adapting and thriving despite adversity.

In summary, surviving extreme conditions demands knowledge, preparation, and adaptability. Understanding the environment, utilizing available resources, and maintaining a resilient mindset are critical to overcoming the challenges of the harshest environments. As we move forward, the ability to adapt to various environments underscores the importance of versatility and ingenuity in wilderness survival.

Adapting to Different Environments

The environment around you can be as unpredictable as beautiful. Adapting to different environments is not just about survival; it's about understanding the natural world and how to coexist. Whether you find yourself in dense forests, arid deserts, icy tundras, or along coastlines, each setting requires unique skills and knowledge to navigate successfully.

In dense forests, the canopy provides shelter, limits visibility, and makes navigation challenging. To adapt, focus on learning how to read the natural signs for direction—moss growth, sun position, and the behavior of water streams can guide you. Building a shelter in such an environment often means utilizing the abundant materials around you, like branches and leaves, to create insulation and protection from the elements.

Deserts present a stark contrast, where water scarcity and extreme temperature fluctuations are often the primary concern. In these environments, conserving energy and moisture becomes paramount. Travel during the cooler hours of the early morning or late evening to avoid the harshest heat. Use clothing to shield your skin from the sun and retain moisture. Finding water may require knowledge of extracting moisture from plants or locating hidden sources underground.

The cold is relentless in icy tundras, and the landscape may seem barren. However, snow and ice can be both a challenge and a resource. Building a snow shelter can protect you from the wind and insulate against the cold. Understanding how to move safely across the ice, recognizing signs of hypothermia, and finding food sources are critical skills. Fire-making is essential, not just for warmth but for melting snow for water.

Coastal environments offer a bounty of resources but also unique hazards. Learning how to source fresh water, either through collection methods or by identifying freshwater streams, is crucial. The sea can provide food, but knowledge of local marine life and tides is necessary to avoid danger. Shelter might need to account for changing tides and the potential for damp conditions.

In each of these environments, the principles of survival remain constant: find shelter, water, and food and maintain a positive mental attitude. However, the methods by which you achieve these needs can vary dramatically. Adapting to different environments is about flexibility, observation, and a willingness to learn from the natural world. It's about making the environment work for you, using its resources wisely, and respecting its limits.

As we move forward, remember that protecting yourself from the elements is not just about immediate survival. It's about planning, preparation, and understanding the nuanced interplay between the weather and your environment. Whether it's the scorching sun, the pouring rain, or the biting cold, each element presents challenges and opportunities for the knowledgeable survivor.

Impact of Climate Change on Survival

The elements are not just a backdrop to our adventures; they are dynamic forces that shape our experiences, challenge our skills, and test our resilience. As the planet warms, the impact of climate change on these natural elements becomes increasingly significant, altering the very fabric of wilderness survival. Understanding these changes is not just about staying ahead in the survival game; it's about adapting to a rapidly changing world where the rules of engagement with nature are constantly rewritten.

Climate change has led to more extreme weather patterns, including increased temperatures, intense storms, and unpredictable weather events. These changes affect the environment and the strategies needed for survival in the wilderness. For instance, higher temperatures can lead to dehydration and heatstroke, making water sourcing and cooling techniques paramount. Meanwhile, the increased frequency and intensity of storms demand improved shelter-building skills and the ability to predict weather changes accurately.

Moreover, climate change impacts the availability and distribution of resources. Shifts in climate zones affect the habitats of plants and animals, altering the availability of food and materials in certain areas. For example, as temperatures rise, some plant species that survivalists might rely on for food or medicine are moving to higher elevations or latitudes. Similarly, animal migration patterns are changing, affecting hunting and trapping. Adapting to these shifts requires a deeper understanding of local ecosystems and the flexibility to adjust traditional survival techniques.

The melting of snow and ice is another critical aspect of climate change affecting wilderness survival. In regions where ice fishing, snow shelter construction, or glacier navigation were once standard survival practices, the changing conditions demand new skills and knowledge. For instance, thinner ice presents new dangers for crossing frozen lakes, requiring more sophisticated techniques to assess ice safety.

Rising sea levels and the increased acidity of oceans and freshwater sources pose additional challenges, especially in coastal areas. Saltwater intrusion can make finding potable water more complex, and the changing composition of aquatic ecosystems can affect the availability of fish and other marine resources.

To navigate these challenges, survivalists must become students of the environment, continuously learning and adapting. This means honing traditional survival skills and integrating new knowledge about climate change and its effects. It involves staying informed about the latest scientific findings, understanding the local impacts of global changes, and developing a versatile skill set that can be adapted to various conditions.

In conclusion, the impact of climate change on wilderness survival is profound and multifaceted. It challenges us to rethink our strategies and adapt our skills to a changing world. By embracing this challenge, we can become more resilient, resourceful, and in tune with the natural world, ensuring that we can thrive in the wilderness, no matter what the future holds.

Chapter Summary

- Understanding and predicting weather patterns, involving traditional methods and modern technology, is crucial for survival in the wilderness.
- Cloud formations, animal behavior, and plant reactions indicate impending weather changes.
- Modern tools like portable weather radios and smartphone apps aid in weather

prediction. However, their effectiveness can be limited in remote areas.
- Survival in extreme conditions requires knowledge of shelter construction, hydration management, and food sourcing specific to the environment.
- Psychological resilience and physical preparation are crucial in surviving harsh conditions.
- Adapting to different environments (forests, deserts, tundras, coastlines) requires unique skills and knowledge for each setting.
- Protecting oneself from the elements involves creating shelters, understanding wind, harnessing fire, layering for temperature regulation, staying dry, sun protection, and hydration strategies.
- Climate change impacts wilderness survival by altering weather patterns and resource availability and requiring new survival strategies and adaptability to changing conditions.

9

SURVIVAL PSYCHOLOGY

Three adventurers surviving in the wild.

Staying Calm Under Pressure

In the wilderness, the unexpected is the only guarantee. You might feel immense pressure rapidly if faced with a sudden storm, a lost path, or dwindling supplies. In these moments, when the stakes are highest, staying calm under pressure becomes your most crucial survival skill. This section delves into practical strategies to maintain composure and make rational decisions, even when every instinct might be urging you to panic.

First and foremost, acknowledge your feelings. Fear, anxiety, and stress are natural responses to threatening situations. Recognizing these emotions without judgment allows you to assess them objectively and prevents them from overwhelming your thought process. Remember, your goal is not to eliminate these feelings but to manage them effectively.

Breathing techniques are a powerful tool in regaining control over your emotional state. Deep, controlled breaths can help reduce stress levels and improve cognitive function. Remember the "4-7-8" technique from Chapter 5?

1. Inhale deeply through your nose for 4 seconds.
2. Hold your breath for 7 seconds.
3. Exhale slowly through your mouth for 8 seconds.

This method calms the nervous system and encourages a moment of pause to assess your situation more clearly.

Visualization is another effective strategy. Imagine yourself successfully navigating the challenge at hand. This not only boosts confidence but also helps in formulating a practical plan of action. Visualization primes the brain for success, making you more likely to achieve the outcome you're focusing on.

Maintaining a positive attitude is crucial. It's easy to spiral into despair when faced with adversity, but positivity can be a powerful motivator. Focus on what you can control rather than what you can't. Celebrate small victories, no matter how minor they may seem. These moments of success build momentum and reinforce your belief in overcoming obstacles.

Lastly, prioritize tasks to avoid feeling overwhelmed. Break down your situation into manageable actions. Ask yourself, "What's the most important thing I need to do right now?" By focusing on one task at a time, you can maintain a sense of control and progress, which is essential for staying calm under pressure.

In wilderness survival, as in life, staying calm under pressure can make the difference between success and failure. By mastering these techniques, you equip yourself with the mental resilience to face any challenge head-on. Remember, the wilderness does not discriminate; it is unforgiving to panic but rewarding to preparedness and composure.

The Will to Survive

The will to survive becomes a psychological concept and a tangible force that can mean the difference between life and death. This section delves into the essence of this will, exploring how it shapes our actions, decisions, and, ultimately, our survival in the wild.

Survival psychology posits that the will to survive is intrinsic to human nature, yet it manifests differently in each individual. It's a complex interplay of mental, emotional, and physical factors that can be nurtured and strengthened over time. Understanding and harnessing this will is crucial for anyone battling the elements, far from the comforts and safety of civilization.

One of the first steps in cultivating a strong will to survive is recognizing the power of positive thinking. In adversity, the mind can be your greatest ally or worst enemy. Negative thoughts can spiral into despair, panic, or resignation, which can hasten defeat. Conversely, maintaining a positive outlook can inspire creativity, resilience, and the determination to overcome obstacles. It's about focusing on one's goals, not the hurdles, and believing in one's ability to prevail.

Another critical aspect is motivation. This can come from the desire to reunite with loved ones, the responsibility to provide for a family or even the personal challenge of testing one's limits. Identifying this motivation is crucial, as it serves as a beacon of hope, a constant reminder of why it's essential to keep pushing forward, even when the situation seems impossible.

Preparation and knowledge also play significant roles in strengthening the will to survive. The more skilled and informed one is about survival techniques, the more confident and mentally prepared one will be when facing challenges. This confidence boosts morale and fosters a proactive attitude, essential for survival. It's about transforming fear into focus, channeling energy into constructive actions rather than allowing panic to consume and immobilize.

Adaptability is another critical component. The wilderness is ever-changing, and survival often hinges on adapting to new challenges and environments. This requires flexibility in thinking, the willingness to learn from mistakes, and the creativity to devise novel solutions. It's a testament to the human spirit's capacity to endure and evolve in adversity.

Lastly, the will to survive is deeply connected to the human instinct for connection and support. Even in solitude, the thought of loved ones or the prospect of returning to them can provide immense psychological strength. In group situations, collective will and mutual support can amplify individual efforts, creating a powerful synergy that enhances the chances of survival for everyone involved.

In conclusion, the will to survive is a multifaceted force shaped by mindset, motivation, preparation, adaptability, and human connection. It's about harnessing the power of the mind, body, and spirit to face the unknown with courage, determination, and hope. As we move forward, understanding how to make decisions in crises becomes the next critical step, building on the foundation of a strong will to survive.

Decision-Making in Crisis Situations

Every decision can mean the difference between survival and peril. When faced with a crisis, making sound, timely decisions becomes paramount. This section delves into the critical aspects of decision-making in crises, offering practical advice to navigate the complexities of survival psychology.

First and foremost, it's essential to maintain a calm demeanor. Panic is the archenemy of rational decision-making. When you find yourself in a crisis, take a deep breath and assess your situation with as much objectivity as possible. This moment of pause allows your brain to switch from reactive to proactive, enabling you to evaluate your options more clearly.

Next, prioritize your needs. In a survival situation, your primary concerns should be shelter, water, fire, and food, in that order. This hierarchy of needs can guide your decision-making process, helping you focus on what's most critical at any given moment. For instance, if you're lost in a cold environment, finding or creating shelter to protect yourself from the elements becomes your top priority.

Another critical aspect of decision-making in the wilderness is gathering information. Before making any decisions, try to collect as much data about your surroundings and situation as possible. This could involve observing the sun's position to determine direction, checking your supplies to know what you have at your disposal, or scouting your immediate area for resources or hazards. Armed with this information, you can make more informed decisions that increase your chances of survival.

Setting realistic goals and breaking them down into manageable tasks is also crucial. Instead of fixating on the end goal of being rescued, focus on what you can achieve right now. Whether building a shelter, starting a fire, or signaling for help, each small victory can boost your morale and propel you forward.

Lastly, be prepared to adapt. The wilderness is unpredictable, and what works in one situation may not work in another. Flexibility and the willingness to change your plan as new information becomes available are vital components of effective decision-making in crises.

Understanding and applying these principles can enhance your ability to make sound decisions when it matters most. Remember, your mind is your most valuable survival tool in the wilderness. Cultivating strong decision-making skills can help you navigate the challenges of the wild but also enrich your everyday life with greater resilience and adaptability.

Group Dynamics and Leadership

The psychological aspect of survival often becomes as crucial as the practical skills of finding shelter, water, and food. Within this realm of survival psychology, understanding group dynamics and leadership can significantly influence the outcome of a survival situation. This section delves into the intricacies of how groups function in extreme conditions and the pivotal role of leadership in navigating the challenges that arise.

When individuals are in a survival scenario as part of a group, the initial reaction can range from panic to denial. During these first moments, the foundation for group dynamics is laid. A group's ability to organize, allocate resources, and make collective decisions can mean the difference between despair and hope. The key to this organization often lies in the emergence of leadership.

Leadership in a wilderness survival context only sometimes follows conventional norms. The most physically strong or vocally assertive individual is only sometimes the best leader. Instead, effective leadership often emerges from those who can maintain calm, think clearly under pressure, and possess relevant survival skills. A leader's ability to inspire confidence, foster cooperation, and maintain morale becomes their most valuable asset.

However, leadership is more than just one person taking charge. It also involves recognizing the strengths and weaknesses within the group and delegating tasks accordingly. A leader who can empower others to contribute meaningfully optimizes the group's chances of survival and helps maintain a positive group dynamic. This collaborative approach can prevent conflict and ensure that decisions are made considering the group's best interests.

Communication plays a critical role in maintaining effective group dynamics. In the silence of the wilderness, transparent and open communication can prevent misunderstandings and ensure that everyone is aware of the group's plans and objectives. A leader must facilitate this communication, encouraging everyone to voice their thoughts and concerns. This inclusivity can bolster group cohesion and resilience in the face of adversity.

Yet, leadership in survival situations has its challenges. The stress and strain of the environment can lead to tension and conflict within the group. A leader must navigate these interpersonal dynamics with sensitivity and assertiveness, addressing issues before they escalate and threaten the group's unity. It is a delicate balance between maintaining authority and fostering mutual respect.

In conclusion, the dynamics of group behavior and the essence of leadership in wilderness survival are complex and multifaceted. A group's ability to organize itself, with a leader who can effectively harness its collective strengths, significantly enhances its survival prospects. As we move forward, understanding the psychological underpinnings of these dynamics can equip individuals with the knowledge to face the wilderness not just as a collection of individuals but as a unified entity with a shared goal of survival. This understanding of group dynamics and leadership serves as a bridge to navigating the emotional and psychological challenges posed by isolation and fear, further emphasizing the interconnectedness of survival psychology.

Coping with Isolation and Fear

In the wilderness, the challenges extend beyond the physical to include significant psychological hurdles, such as dealing with isolation and fear. These emotions can become overwhelming, mainly when separated from their group or alone in an unfamiliar setting. However, learning to manage these feelings is crucial for survival. Here are several effective strategies for overcoming the psychological challenges of isolation and fear.

Accepting your situation is the first step toward

overcoming any challenge. Recognize and accept your feelings of fear and isolation without judgment, understanding that it's a natural response to uncertainty. This acceptance allows you to focus on constructive actions rather than being immobilized by fear.

Keeping busy is essential. An idle mind can exacerbate fear and negative thoughts, so engage in survival-related tasks such as building a shelter, gathering food, or creating signals for rescue. These activities improve your chances of survival and give you a sense of purpose and accomplishment, which can be uplifting in difficult times.

Establishing a routine can introduce a sense of normalcy to your situation. Set specific times for various tasks, including foraging, resting, and shelter maintenance. This structure helps maintain focus and reduces feelings of aimlessness and despair.

Mindfulness and meditation are powerful tools for managing fear and anxiety. Dedicate time each day to sit quietly, breathe deeply, and observe your surroundings without judgment. This practice can ground you in the present moment, alleviating feelings of isolation and fear.

Visualization of positive outcomes, a technique widely used by athletes and successful individuals, can also be beneficial. Regularly imagine yourself being rescued or finding your way back to safety. These positive visualizations can enhance morale and motivation, keeping spirits high even in challenging situations.

Connecting with nature can also provide comfort. While isolation can be challenging, it offers a unique opportunity to connect with the natural world. Appreciate the beauty around you, whether it's the sound of a stream, the sight of wildlife, or the sun's warmth. This connection can create a sense of belonging and peace, reducing feelings of loneliness.

Keeping a journal allows you to express your thoughts and experiences constructively. Documenting your journey can offer valuable insights and remind you of your resilience and strength.

Most importantly, maintain hope. Remember why you're striving to survive and the loved ones awaiting your return. Hope is a powerful motivator that can drive you to persevere through the most challenging times.

Addressing the mind and body is essential when coping with isolation and fear in the wilderness. By implementing these strategies, you can preserve your psychological well-being, significantly improving your chances of survival. Survival is as much about mental resilience as it is about physical endurance.

Chapter Summary

- Acknowledge feelings of fear and anxiety without judgment to manage them effectively and prevent them from overwhelming your thought process.
- Use breathing techniques, like the "4-7-8" method, to reduce stress and improve cognitive function, helping to maintain composure in stressful situations.
- Employ visualization to boost confidence and formulate practical action plans, priming the brain for success.
- Maintain a positive attitude, focusing on controllable aspects and celebrating small victories to build momentum and belief in overcoming obstacles.
- Prioritize tasks to avoid feeling overwhelmed, breaking down situations into manageable actions to maintain control and progress.
- Cultivate a solid will to survive by focusing on positive thinking, identifying motivation, preparing with knowledge, adapting to changes, and valuing human connections.

- Enhance decision-making skills in crisis by staying calm, prioritizing needs, gathering information, setting realistic goals, and being prepared to adapt.
- Navigate group dynamics and leadership in survival situations by organizing, utilizing effective communication, recognizing individual strengths, and maintaining group cohesion and morale.

10

ADVANCED SURVIVAL TECHNIQUES

An explorer creating a fireplace.

Improvised Weapons and Tools

Creating improvised weapons and tools from the natural environment can be a critical survival skill in the wilderness. This section delves into the art of crafting essential tools and weapons using only what nature provides, ensuring you're prepared for both the challenges of survival and the necessity of self-defense.

Crafting Improvised Weapons

1. **Spears:** A spear can be made by sharpening a long, straight stick. A rock or bone can be shaped and attached to the tip for a more durable point. Spears are helpful for hunting and can serve as a defensive weapon against predators.
2. **Slingshots:** A Y-shaped branch, coupled with a rubber band or tire's inner tube, can be transformed into a slingshot. Small rocks or metal pieces serve as effective ammunition. This weapon is handy for small-game hunting.
3. **Bows and Arrows:** Crafting a bow and arrow requires more time and skill but is highly effective for hunting from a distance. Flexible wood, string, and feathered arrows are the components of this classic survival weapon.

Creating Essential Tools

1. **Knives:** A sharp stone, flint, or even a piece of bone can be fashioned into a cutting tool. These improvised knives are crucial for preparing food, crafting other tools, and various survival tasks.
2. **Axes:** A larger stone attached to a sturdy stick can serve as an improvised axe. This tool is invaluable for chopping wood for fire or shelter construction.
3. **Fishing Gear:** You can assemble adequate fishing gear using natural fibers to create a line and shape bone or wood into hooks. Additionally, nets can be woven from vines or plant fibers.

Maintenance and Safety

Maintaining your improvised weapons and tools is essential to remain functional and practical. Regular inspection is crucial in identifying any wear and tear or damage that could compromise their performance. By dedicating time to repair and upkeep, you can extend the lifespan of your equipment, ensuring it is ready and reliable when you need it most. This proactive maintenance approach saves resources and ensures that your tools and weapons perform optimally.

Safety should always be prioritized when handling and storing improvised weapons and tools. It is essential to familiarize yourself with the proper handling techniques for each piece of equipment. This includes understanding how to safely use, transport, and store them to minimize the risk of accidental injury to yourself or others. Implementing safe practices can prevent unnecessary accidents and ensure that your tools and weapons are preserved in good condition for future use.

In addition to regular maintenance and practicing safe handling, creating a designated storage area for your tools and weapons can further enhance safety. This area should be secure, organized, and, ideally, accessible only to those trained and authorized to use the equipment. By keeping your tools and weapons in a designated area, you reduce the risk of them being mishandled or used by untrained individuals. This organized approach not only contributes to the overall safety of your environment but also helps maintain the condition and readiness of your equipment.

In conclusion, mastering the art of creating improvised weapons and tools is a testament to human ingenuity and adaptability. These skills enhance your chances of survival and deepen your connection with the natural world. As you progress in your wilderness survival journey, remember that the environment around you is rich with resources—each with the potential to aid your survival.

Constructing Long-Term Shelters

Mastering the construction of long-term shelters is a crucial skill in wilderness survival, going beyond the basics of creating a temporary refuge. This involves understanding the specific environment, as different climates and terrains necessitate different shelter types. For example, a dense forest environment would benefit from the abundant wood for construction. In contrast, a desert environment would require a focus on insulation and shade.

The first step in building a long-term shelter is selecting an appropriate site. It's essential to find a flat, well-drained area sheltered from prevailing winds and close to a water source yet not prone to flooding. The site should also be safe from hazards like falling branches or wildlife paths.

The materials for the shelter depend on what's available in the surroundings. In wooded areas, fallen branches, leaves, and moss are helpful, while in more barren landscapes, rocks, earth, and any repurposable human-made materials might be necessary. Tools can range from simple knives or hatchets to more sophisticated tools brought with or improvised from the environment.

Constructing a long-term shelter typically starts with building a sturdy frame from larger branches or logs, using lashing techniques with vines or makeshift ropes for security. Insulating the walls and roof with materials like leaves, grass, or snow is crucial, and the entrance should be positioned away from the wind. Incorporating a fireplace or stove can provide warmth.

For a shelter to be sustainable long-term, it must be sturdy and capable of being repaired and improved over time. Enhancing insulation, ensuring proper drainage, and constructing simple furniture can make the shelter more comfortable.

Safety is paramount, with regular maintenance to check for wear and tear, safe management of fire, and cleanliness to deter wildlife being critical practices.

Constructing a long-term shelter in the wilderness is an advanced skill that requires patience, ingenuity, and a comprehensive understanding of the environment. By carefully selecting the site, utilizing available materials wisely, and focusing on sustainability and safety, it's possible to create a refuge that protects from the elements and offers a comfortable living space in the wild.

Advanced Navigation Challenges

Navigating the wilderness with precision and safety is an essential skill distinguishing between a successful journey and getting lost. This guide explores advanced navigation challenges encountered in the wild and how to tackle them using traditional and modern techniques. These methods are crucial for survival and enhance the outdoor experience by fostering a deeper connection with nature.

A topographical map is an invaluable tool in the wilderness, detailing the area's physical features, including elevations. Learning how to read contour lines, identify landmarks, and understand the map's scale is essential. Combining this knowledge with a compass enables confident navigation through unfamiliar terrain. Practicing triangulation, which involves identifying three known locations on your map and using your compass to find the bearings from your current location to these points, is a critical skill, especially when GPS is not an option.

When a compass is unavailable, the natural environment offers alternative navigation aids. The sun's path, star movements, and even tree moss growth patterns can indicate direction. For example, in the Northern Hemisphere, the sun rises in the east and sets in the west, with noon in the southern sky. At night, the North Star (Polaris) points north. These natural cues help maintain a general sense of direction.

While traditional navigation skills are indispensable, modern technology like GPS devices and satellite messengers can enhance navigation and safety. However, using these tools judiciously is crucial, ensuring spare batteries or power sources are at hand and not relying solely on technology, as devices can fail or lose signal.

Different environments present unique navigation challenges. Dense forests, steep terrains, and vast deserts each require tailored strategies. For instance, dense forests limit visibility and make landmarks harder to spot, necessitating close attention to maps and compasses and using short, precise journey segments to stay oriented. In contrast, deserts offer long-distance visibility of landmarks, though distances can be deceptive due to clear air. Accurately estimating distances and using the sun's position are crucial to desert navigation.

Developing a mental map and maintaining situational awareness is also vital. This involves continuously observing the environment, noting landmarks, and mentally updating your position. Anticipating potential hazards and planning routes accordingly is part of this proactive navigation approach, keeping you oriented and enhancing your wilderness experience.

Mastering these advanced navigation challenges prepares you to explore the wilderness safely and confidently. Whether employing a map and compass, utilizing natural indicators, or integrating modern technology, preparation and practice are essential. Navigation is about reaching your destination and understanding and connecting with the natural world around you.

Living Off the Land

The ability to live off the land is a fundamental skill that ensures sustenance and fosters a deeper connection with nature. As we build on our advanced navigation skills, we rely on the natural resources around us for survival. This guide is designed to provide you with practical and innovative strategies to make the most of the wilderness's bounty.

To start, developing a thorough understanding of your surroundings is crucial. Different ecosystems, from forests and mountains to deserts and coastal areas, offer a variety of resources for survival. Each environment has its unique set of plants, animals, and other materials that can be used for food, water, and shelter. An essential field guide to the local flora and fauna can be invaluable.

Foraging for food is a crucial survival skill, requiring both knowledge and caution. It's essential to distinguish between edible and toxic plants, and familiarizing yourself with the universal edibility test can help determine the safety of unknown plants. Besides plants, insects and small game can also provide nutrition. Techniques such as setting snares or fishing with improvised gear can be effective. Still, being aware of local regulations and ethical considerations is essential.

Water is a critical resource, and finding a reliable source is a top priority. Natural formations that collect rainwater, streams, or even morning dew on vegetation can be water sources. However, any water found must be purified to prevent waterborne diseases, with boiling being the most effective method. Solar water disinfection (SODIS) or makeshift filters can also be used without fire-making tools.

Building a shelter is crucial for protection against the elements. The type of shelter will depend on the available resources and environmental conditions, ranging from lean-tos made of branches to snow caves. The shelter should be sturdy, insulated from the cold ground, and offer protection from the elements.

As you hone your skills in living off the land, it's important to practice sustainability. Taking only what you need, respecting wildlife, and leaving no trace are principles that ensure the preservation of the environment and the availability of resources for future survival needs.

Integrating these survival skills with your knowledge of navigation and self-rescue prepares you for a comprehensive survival strategy, enabling you to thrive in the wilderness. Remember, adaptability is critical. The land provides us with the tools for survival; it's our responsibility to learn how to use them effectively. With practice, patience, and respect for nature, living off the land can become a means of survival and a rewarding way of life.

Self-Rescue Strategies

Exploring the essentials of living off the land is crucial. Still, it's equally important to understand the strategies that could save your life if lost or stranded in the wilderness. Self-rescue strategies go beyond merely finding your way back to civilization; they involve making informed decisions to increase your chances of survival and rescue. These strategies are considered advanced not because they require special skills but because they demand higher awareness, preparation, and mental fortitude.

Making yourself visible to rescuers is a critical first step in self-rescue. This can be achieved by using both natural and human-made materials to create signals that are visible or audible from a distance. Placing brightly colored clothing or materials in open areas, using mirrors or any reflective surface to catch the sun's rays, and lighting fires at night can all serve as effective signals. It's important to remember that three of anything, such as fires, blasts on a whistle, or flashes of light, is universally recognized as a distress signal.

Basic navigation skills can mean the difference between aimlessly wandering and moving towards safety. It's beneficial to know how to use a compass and maps. Still, in their absence, natural indicators like the sun's position, the movement of stars, and the growth patterns of moss on trees can guide you. The goal is to move purposefully and conserve energy for the journey ahead.

Suppose you're near a body of water. In that case, constructing a makeshift raft or learning to navigate rivers can significantly improve your mobility and chances of being found, as water bodies often lead to populated areas. However, it's essential to be aware of the risks, including hypothermia and swift currents.

Leaving markers or a trail for rescuers to follow can also increase your chances of being found. This can be done by tying pieces of fabric to branches, stacking rocks, or drawing arrows in the dirt, aiming to leave a clear path to your current location.

In some situations, the best strategy might be to stay put, especially if you're injured, have limited mobility, or are in an area that meets your basic needs. In such cases, making your location visible and conserving energy are crucial and focusing your signaling efforts to ensure rescuers can find you.

Psychological resilience is the most critical aspect of self-rescue. The will to survive, staying calm under pressure, and the determination to keep going against the odds ultimately define a survivor. Mindfulness and stress management techniques can help maintain a clear head and a hopeful heart.

In the wilderness, every decision can significantly impact your survival. By employing these self-rescue strategies, you're actively participating in your survival, not just waiting to be found. With the proper knowledge and mindset, you can navigate out of challenging situations and back to safety.

Chapter Summary

- Crafting improvised weapons like spears, slingshots, bows, and arrows can be essential for hunting and self-defense in the wilderness.
- Essential tools such as knives, axes, and fishing gear can be made from natural materials for survival tasks like food preparation and shelter construction.
- Regular maintenance and safe handling of improvised weapons and tools are crucial to ensure their functionality and prevent accidents.
- Constructing long-term shelters requires understanding the environment, selecting a suitable site, and using available materials for construction and insulation.
- Advanced navigation challenges in the wilderness can be tackled using traditional methods like maps and compasses, natural indicators, and modern technology.

- Living off the land involves foraging, hunting, finding water, and building shelters with sustainability and respect for nature in mind.
- Self-rescue strategies include making oneself visible to rescuers, navigating purposefully, leaving markers, and maintaining psychological resilience.
- The skills to create improvised tools, navigate challenging terrains, live sustainably off the land, and execute self-rescue strategies are vital for wilderness survival.

THE JOURNEY AHEAD

A survivalist in the wilderness.

Reflecting on What We've Learned

As we pause to reflect on the journey we've embarked upon together, we must recognize the breadth and depth of knowledge we've explored in the realm of wilderness survival. Our exploration has been comprehensive and enlightening, from the foundational skills necessary for any outdoor adventure to the advanced techniques that could mean the difference between life and death in extreme situations.

In traversing this vast landscape of survival wisdom, we've equipped ourselves with practical hacks and strategies and fostered a deeper appreciation for the natural world and our place within it. The skills we've discussed are not merely tools for survival; they are invitations to engage more fully with the environment, to understand its rhythms and nuances, and to respect its power and beauty.

The journey of learning is, by its very nature, unending. Each experience in the wilderness offers new lessons, and each challenge faced provides opportunities for growth and reflection. The knowledge we've acquired is a solid foundation, but it is just the beginning. The actual test of our understanding comes not from mastering the techniques in theory but from applying them in the unpredictable and often unforgiving theater of the great outdoors.

As we move forward, it's crucial to remain curious, open-minded, and willing to continue our education in wilderness survival. The landscape of survival knowledge is as dynamic as the environments it pertains to, with new insights, techniques, and technologies constantly emerging. Staying informed about these developments is a matter of personal interest and a fundamental aspect of responsible wilderness exploration.

Moreover, practicing these skills in real-life scenarios, whether during planned expeditions or unexpected situations, will refine our abilities and deepen our understanding. Each outing is an opportunity to test our knowledge, assess our preparedness, and learn from our successes and setbacks.

In embracing continuous learning, we also open ourselves to the broader community of wilderness enthusiasts and survival experts. Sharing experiences, exchanging tips, and learning from others' perspectives enrich our understanding and contribute to a collective pool of knowledge that benefits all who venture into the natural world.

As we look ahead, let us carry forward the spirit of resilience, adaptability, and respect for nature that has guided our journey thus far. The path of wilderness survival is as much about personal growth and connection with the environment as it is about overcoming challenges. By continuing to educate ourselves and embrace the lessons the wilderness has to teach, we ensure that our adventures are safe, successful, and deeply rewarding.

Continuing Your Survival Education

It's crucial to recognize that the learning journey is only partially complete. The wilderness, with its ever-changing landscapes and unpredictable challenges, demands a continuous commitment to education and skill enhancement. Embracing this ongoing learning process is not just about survival; it's about thriving in the most unexpected circumstances.

Continuing your survival education means seeking new knowledge, techniques, and experiences. The world of wilderness survival is vast, encompassing various environments, each with unique challenges and secrets. From the dense, humid rainforests to the arid expanses of deserts, every environment offers lessons waiting to be learned.

One effective way to continue your education is through practical experience. Regularly put yourself in new and challenging situations within safe and controlled parameters. Whether it's a weekend spent practicing navigation in a local forest or a planned expedition in a more demanding environment, each experience builds upon the last, deepening your understanding and honing your skills.

Another invaluable resource is the knowledge in books, online courses, and workshops. The perspectives and experiences of other survivalists can offer insights that might take years to learn on your own. Diversify your sources of information to include a broad spectrum of environments and survival philosophies. Remember, there's always something new to learn, and someone else's experiences can illuminate aspects of survival you might not have considered.

Engaging with a mentor can also significantly accelerate your learning curve. A mentor with a wealth of experience and knowledge can offer personalized guidance, helping you navigate the complexities of wilderness survival more efficiently. They can provide feedback on your techniques, suggest areas for improvement, and share wisdom that only comes from years of direct experience.

Lastly, embracing the mindset of a lifelong learner is the most crucial aspect of continuing your survival education. Stay curious, open-minded, and willing to leave your comfort zone. The wilderness is a great teacher, offering lessons in resilience, adaptability, and the sheer beauty of the natural world. By committing to an ongoing learning journey, you ensure that you're not just prepared to survive but equipped to thrive, no matter what challenges the wilderness may present.

As we move forward, remember that the wilderness survival community is a vibrant and supportive network eager to welcome new members. Engaging with this community enriches your survival skills. It contributes to the collective knowledge and resilience of those who share your passion for the great outdoors.

Joining the Survivalist Community

As you've journeyed through the realm of wilderness survival, acquiring skills and knowledge to navigate the unpredictable embrace of nature, you're now standing at a pivotal crossroads. Your path has been one of self-discovery, resilience, and an ever-deepening connection with the natural world. Yet, the journey doesn't end here. It's time to consider how you can continue to grow and prepare for your own adventures and contribute to and benefit from a larger community of like-minded individuals. This is where joining the survivalist community comes into play.

The survivalist community is a vibrant and diverse network of individuals who share a common passion for wilderness survival, self-sufficiency, and a profound respect for nature. By becoming part of this community, you open doors to a wealth of knowledge, experience, and camaraderie that can enrich your survival skills and deepen your appreciation for the wild.

Engaging with the survivalist community can take many forms. Online forums and social media groups offer a platform to connect with fellow enthusiasts from around the globe. Here, you can share your own experiences, learn from others' adventures and misadventures, and find answers to questions you might not have even known to ask. These digital spaces are treasure troves of information where the community's collective wisdom is just a few clicks away.

Local clubs and organizations provide another avenue to immerse yourself in the survivalist culture. Participating in workshops, meetups, and expeditions can offer hands-on experience and the opportunity to forge real-world connections with individuals who share your interests. These interactions can be invaluable, providing mentorship, friendship, and the chance to learn and practice skills in a supportive environment.

Moreover, joining the survivalist community isn't just about what you can learn from others; it's also about what you can contribute. Your unique experiences, insights, and skills are valuable to the community. Whether sharing a novel survival hack you've discovered, offering advice based on your personal experiences, or volunteering to lead a workshop, your contributions can help others on their survival journey.

As you consider joining the survivalist community, remember that it's a step towards enhancing your survival skills and building a more resilient, knowledgeable, and connected network of wilderness enthusiasts. It's about being part of something larger than yourself. This community values the lessons learned in the embrace of nature. It is committed to preserving and respecting the wild spaces that inspire us all.

So, as you prepare for your next adventure, think about how you can engage with the survivalist community. Whether through online platforms, local groups, or even starting your initiative, your participation can enrich your wilderness journey in ways you've yet to imagine. The path ahead is not just about surviving; it's about thriving, learning, and sharing in the collective wisdom of a community that shares your passion for the wild.

Preparing for Your Next Adventure

Standing on the brink of your next wilderness adventure, it's essential to recognize that thorough preparation is the cornerstone of surviving and thriving in the great outdoors. The journey you're about to embark on requires as much mental and physical readiness as it does enthusiasm for the unpredictability of nature. Consider these vital tips to ensure you're well-prepared for whatever challenges you might face.

Firstly, commit to continuous learning. The realm of wilderness survival is broad and constantly changing. Keep yourself updated with the latest survival techniques, gear advancements, and environmental changes by reading books, taking online courses, and attending workshops. This ongoing education will keep your survival knowledge up-to-date.

Next, make sure to inspect and update your gear before you leave. Check your tools, shelter, sleeping equipment, and the expiration dates on your first aid supplies and food. This is also an excellent time to consider investing in new gear to enhance your safety and comfort during your adventure.

Physical preparation cannot be overlooked. Wilderness survival demands a lot from your body, so regular exercise that improves cardiovascular health, strength, and flexibility is crucial. Design your fitness routine to reflect the activities you'll be doing, such as hiking, climbing, or paddling, to prepare your body for the challenges ahead better.

Mental resilience is the most critical aspect of your preparation. The wilderness can be as mentally taxing as it is physically—practice stress management techniques like mindfulness or meditation to bolster your mental toughness. Being calm and thinking clearly under pressure can significantly impact your survival.

Gaining practical experience is invaluable. Test your skills in controlled settings by participating in survival workshops, joining outdoor clubs, or planning short trips. These experiences are excellent teachers, providing insights and building confidence that only come from practice.

Always have a detailed plan for your adventure, including your route, expected return times, and backup plans. It's equally important to inform someone you trust about your plans so that they know where to look for you if something goes wrong.

Lastly, embrace the survivalist mindset, which emphasizes adaptability, resilience, and a profound respect for nature. Approach each adventure with humility and an eagerness to learn from the environment and your experiences.

As you gear up for your next wilderness journey, remember that it's not just about testing your survival skills but also about forging a deeper connection with nature, discovering your strengths, and pushing beyond your limits. With the proper preparation, you're not merely surviving; you're thriving, learning, and evolving into a more skilled and resilient adventurer with each step you take into the wild.

Final Thoughts

As we draw the curtains on this guide, we must reflect on what we've journeyed through together. The wilderness, with its untamed beauty and unpredictable challenges, is a profound metaphor for life. Each survival hack, tip, and anecdote shared within these pages is more than just a means to endure the physical world; they are lessons in resilience, adaptability, and the indomitable human spirit.

The journey ahead, whether it leads you to the heart of dense forests, atop the craggiest peaks, or into the depths of your untapped potential, is ripe with opportunities for growth and discovery. The wilderness survival hacks we've explored are your toolkit, not just for the wilds of nature but for navigating the unpredictable terrains of everyday life.

Remember, one of the most remarkable survival hacks is how you approach challenges. It's about seeing beyond the immediate threat or discomfort and recognizing the opportunities for learning and growth that adversity presents. This mindset, cultivated in the wild, can transform obstacles into stepping stones, leading to personal growth and a deeper appreciation for the world around us.

As you prepare for your next adventure, whether a meticulously planned expedition or the spontaneous call of the wild, carry the knowledge and insights from these pages. Let them guide you in practical survival and living a life filled with adventure, learning, and a relentless pursuit of pushing beyond your limits.

In the end, the journey ahead is yours to shape. Armed with the right skills, a resilient mindset, and an open heart, there's no limit to the adventures you can embark upon. The wilderness awaits a vast, vivid classroom ready to teach its timeless lessons. Embrace it with respect, curiosity, and a readiness to learn, and you'll find that the most incredible survival hack of all is the journey itself.

Your Feedback Matters

Thank you for joining me on this journey. If the book inspired you, please share your thoughts by leaving a review on Amazon using the QR code below. Your feedback is invaluable and helps guide others. I'm grateful for your time and hope the insights you've gained enrich your quest for knowledge.

ABOUT THE AUTHOR

Alfred Gibson is an author and wilderness survival expert, best known for his Wilderness Mastery Essentials series. With extensive experience in survival training and outdoor education, his work focuses on practical survival hacks and bushcraft first aid. Gibson's expertise has made his books essential for outdoor enthusiasts. Beyond writing, he is deeply involved in exploring and testing survival techniques in the wild.

www.ingramcontent.com/pod-product-compliance
Lightning Source LLC
Chambersburg PA
CBHW051548020426
42333CB00016B/2162

emergencies, not just for our sake but to ensure we are not a burden on the natural resources or the local communities that may come to our aid.

The journey ahead in the wilderness, armed with the knowledge of bushcraft first aid, is an invitation to a lifelong learning experience. Each trip is an opportunity to apply what we have learned, make mistakes, grow, and share our experiences with others. It is a chance to strengthen our bond with nature, contribute to preserving these wild spaces, and encourage others to approach the wilderness with the same confidence and respect.

As we close this chapter, let us carry forward the ethos of the ethical wilderness explorer, blending it with the practical skills of bushcraft first aid. Let this knowledge not just be a shield against the adversities of the wild but a bridge that connects us more deeply with the natural world. The journey ahead is not just about surviving the wilderness; it's about thriving within it, learning its secrets, and respecting its power. With each step, let us remember that the most incredible adventures enlighten, challenge, and remind us of our place in the natural order.

Your Feedback Matters

Thank you for joining me on this journey. If the book inspired you, please share your thoughts by leaving a review on Amazon using the QR code below. Your feedback is invaluable and helps guide others. I'm grateful for your time and hope the insights you've gained enrich your quest for knowledge.

ABOUT THE AUTHOR

Alfred Gibson is an author and wilderness survival expert, best known for his Wilderness Mastery Essentials series. With extensive experience in survival training and outdoor education, his work focuses on practical survival hacks and bushcraft first aid. Gibson's expertise has made his books essential for outdoor enthusiasts. Beyond writing, he is deeply involved in exploring and testing survival techniques in the wild.

www.ingramcontent.com/pod-product-compliance
Lightning Source LLC
Chambersburg PA
CBHW051548020426
42333CB00016B/2161